TEACHING READING
as a Language Experience

D1445631

TEACHING READING
as a Language Experience

MaryAnne Hall
University of Maryland

Charles E. Merrill Publishing Company
A Bell & Howell Company
Columbus, Ohio

International Standard Book Number: 0-675-09376-7

Library of Congress Catalogue Card Number: 75-103320

5 75

Printed in the United States of America

Preface

The language experience approach to reading instruction is currently the object of much interest throughout the nation. Reading authorities, supervisory personnel, and classroom teachers are exploring the contributions and advantages of an integrated language arts approach to reading. As teachers seek guidelines for developing reading programs based on the language experience approach, requests have come for information regarding the classroom implementation of this approach. The purpose of this book is to describe this approach and to identify instructional practices which can be followed in teaching reading in the language experience framework.

Communication skills can best be developed in an integrated and functional framework of teaching reading and language skills. Integrating reading instruction with the other language arts has long been a goal of reading programs, and the language experience approach truly illustrates this goal through all classroom reading experiences. The writer feels that teachers should recognize the linguistic nature of the reading process and adapt the instructional practices for teaching reading with an emphasis on communication.

This book *is not* a collection of practices for teaching. However, ideas for teaching are presented as illustrations of the language experience approach in action. This book *is* a description of the theoretical base of the language experience approach and the implementation of this theoretical base in a classroom setting. The practical ideas included are to illustrate the basic philosophy of fostering communication in a creative, personal, and functional way of learning and teaching.

The book is organized in two parts. The first two chapters establish the theoretical background of the language experience approach and its relationship to the total elementary reading and language curriculum. The last seven chapters are concerned with the practical implementation of the language experience approach in the classroom. These chapters discuss experience stories, creative writing, vocabulary development, and literature experiences as well as the teaching of specific pre-reading and reading skills. The final chapter summarizes the information presented and describes an effective setting for the language experience approach.

While this book is devoted exclusively to language experience reading, the reader should not assume that this approach is advocated by the author as the only means for teaching reading or that this approach is without limitations. Informed teachers will utilize practices from a variety of approaches. This source can add to the background of the elementary teacher who wishes to draw upon the language experience framework as one component in a total reading program.

Special thanks goes to the many teachers and teacher-education students who tried and revised some of the procedures described here. Their comments greatly clarified the activities. Grateful appreciation also goes to our photographer Charles Bohn and to Susan Crowley and Betty Berson for their patient and thorough typing and retyping of the manuscript.

MaryAnne Hall

Contents

TEACHING READING
as a Language Experience

CHAPTER ONE

The Nature of the Language Experience Approach

Reading is a language-based process which is used for the transmission of meaning through the interpretation of printed symbols. The complex process of reading includes the decoding of print, the association of meaning with the printed symbols, and the reaction of the reader as he associates an author's meaning with his previous knowledge. Reading skill is dependent upon language facility, but in some approaches to teaching reading, the relationship between reading and language has not been an influential force affecting instructional practices. However, in recent years greater recognition has been directed to emphasizing the linguistic and communicative nature of the reading process in the teaching of reading. One approach to teaching reading, the language experience approach, is based on the interrelatedness of language and reading. Pupils learn to read in a communication context where reading occurs in conjunction with talking, listening, and writing.

Language plays a primary role in the life of an individual since it is the medium that makes communication with others in the social environment possible. The acquisition of language by young children is a complex developmental task which involves symbolic learning in order to formulate, express, and receive meaning. The development and refinement of the ability to communicate through effective use of language is a major

1

concern in the elementary school curriculum. Shane comments on the significance of promoting language development.

> It seems an inescapable conclusion that an important reason for emphasizing language *skills* is that language power serves to under-gird the future academic progress of children more than does any other single asset that a boy or girl can develop. Teachers will also wish to remember that fluency in language—that is, highly developed word power—is the one measurable quality which seems to be shared by leaders in adult life, whether they are industrialists, soldiers, statesmen, or professional men. Success in school and in becoming a contributive adult is undoubtedly related to linguistic ability.[1]

RELATIONSHIP BETWEEN READING AND ORAL LANGUAGE

Oral language and reading are closely related. Linguists tell us that speech is the primary form of language and that written language is an imperfect representation of speech. Research confirms that children's achievement in oral and written language is related. Ruddell states:

> The research and opinion would suggest that an instructional program designed to develop an understanding of the relationship between the child's familiar spoken system of communication and written language would facilitate his abilty to comprehend written material.[2]

Some common elements of symbolization and concept development are required for effective use of both oral and written language. Children learn the spoken symbol system of language before learning the graphic symbol system involved in writing and reading. Facility with oral language is one important determinant of success in reading. Dechant explains: "In our language, reading requires the child to see mentally the oral

---

[1] Harold G. Shane *et al.*, *Improving Language Arts Instruction in the Elementary School* (Columbus, Ohio: Charles E. Merrill Publishing Company, 1962), p. 11.

[2] Robert B. Ruddell, "Reading Instruction in First Grade With Varying Emphasis on the Regularity of Grapheme-Phoneme Correspondences and the Relation of Language Structure to Meaning—Extended into Second Grade," *The Reading Teacher*, XX (May, 1967), 731.

counterparts of the printed symbols. Only after he has done this does he respond with meaning to the symbol."[3]

Both reading and listening require the interpretation of verbal symbols although in one case the symbols are recognized auditorially while in the other the symbols are recognized visually. Lefevre writes:

> Learning the skills of literacy—reading and writing—requires mastery of a dual set of closely interconnected linguistic patterns that are much alike but also greatly different from each other. Thus learning the language arts involves grasping the interrelationships of two distinct and separate yet closely related symbol systems for human communication. One system is audio-lingual, a matter of mouth and ear; the other is manual-visual, a matter of hand and eye.[4]

Teachers need to examine the interrelatedness of oral and written language and to capitalize on this interrerlatedness as they teach children to communicate effectively in reading, speaking, listening, and writing. As children listen they are building their stock of words and knowledge. As children speak their powers of communication are sharpened. As they read they are drawing upon their previous knowledge of words and adding new thoughts and concepts.

Language and communication skills require the use of listening and reading to receive ideas and speaking and writing to express thoughts. A teacher must be concerned with developing language power, not just reading ability. Without facility in all the communication skills, the value of reading as a communication process is not fully realized. Attention to interpreting language in listening situations, to formulating thoughts through speech, to interpreting print in reading, and to expressing thoughts in writing are the core of the language program. While in this book the focus is on providing reading experiences in a language experience framework, those experiences cannot be provided outside of a communication context.

In an integrated approach to teaching communication skills, oral language development presents the base for developing skill in decoding and comprehending written language. Reading must be viewed as a linguistic process and must be taught with the focus on the communication process.

---

[3] Emerald V. Dechant, *Improving the Teaching of Reading* (Englewood Cliffs, N. J.: Prentice-Hall, Inc., 1964), p. 85.

[4] Carl A. Lefevre, "Language and Self: Fulfillment of Trauma? Part I," *Elementary English*, XLIII (February, 1966), p. 127.

Four implications of the relationship between oral and written language for teaching reading are:

1. *The language of initial reading materials should represent the child's speech patterns.* In the beginning stages of instruction, reading will have more meaning for children when they learn to read the language patterns and vocabulary already employed in their speech.

2. *Reading instruction should build upon the relationship between spoken and written language.* As children decode printed symbols they relate those symbols to their existing knowledge of speech sounds and vocabulary.

3. *Reading experiences are taught as communication experiences even in the beginning stages.* Communication in reading does not overlook or minimize the importance of phonics and other word attack skills in decoding print. Children must be able to recognize printed words if they are to be successful in reading. However, as children are acquiring a reading vocabulary, the meaning of the material read should be evident to them. In the language experience approach both decoding and communication are included in the reading experiences. (See Chapter 8 for more detailed information on teaching word attack with this approach.)

4. *Reading instruction must be related to the total language program.* As children receive instruction in oral language, this instruction enriches their total background for comprehending the printed language of reading materials. Attention in the total language program is given to vocabulary development, to language enrichment through literature experiences, and to the expression of thoughts in written language.

WHAT IS THE LANGUAGE EXPERIENCE APPROACH?

The language experience approach to reading integrates the teaching of reading with the other language arts as children listen, speak, write, and read about their personal experiences and ideas. A child's speech determines the *language patterns* of the reading materials, and his experiences determine the *content.* This approach is based on the concept that reading has the most meaning to a pupil when the materials being read are expressed in his language and are rooted in his experiences.

As children see their spoken thoughts put into written form they can understand the nature of communication in reading in addition to recognizing words. Communication is stressed as children speak, see the speech represented by printed symbols, and then read the written representation of their speech. The association of meaning with the print is built into the reading of the personally created materials of the language experience approach.

The sequence of communication in the language experience approach can be represented by the following diagram:

DIAGRAM I

The Communication Sequence in the Language Experience Approach

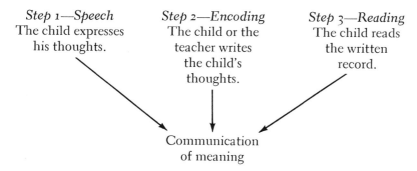

Step 1—Speech
The child expresses
his thoughts.

Step 2—Encoding
The child or the
teacher writes
the child's
thoughts.

Step 3—Reading
The child reads
the written
record.

Communication
of meaning

In the language experience approach, the purpose of communication underlies the three stages of producing reading materials depicted in the above diagram. Diagram I shows the child's involvement as he moves from talking to encoding to the reading of his thoughts. As the child sees his speech encoded into the printed symbols, the communication of the meaning of his speech in written form is evident to him. As he decodes the printed symbols and associates them with his previously spoken thoughts, he is communicating through reading.

Reading is not "talk written down" but instead is the process of decoding and comprehending printed symbols. In the language experience approach, the written record itself may be viewed as "talk written down" but the reading of the written record involves decoding the printed symbols and responding to them with meaningful interpretation.

A limitation of relying on a reader's experiences for developing reading material is that a child may not be able to put all of his experiences into verbal form. However, the language experience approach seeks to broaden experience, provides many opportunities for a child to articulate his experiences, and seeks to develop his power to communicate orally.

A reader should grasp the relationship between speech and written language, yet he should not be led to believe that the English alphabet provides an exact coding system for oral language. In English the relationship between speech sounds and the letter symbols for sounds is not entirely regular since some sounds can be represented by more than one letter and since some letters represent more than one sound. For example, the sound of long e can be represented by the *ea* in *each*, *ee* in *meet*, the *ey* in *key*, and the beginning sound in *kite* and *cow* can be represented by *k* or *c*. Also, speech intonation patterns help communicate the speaker's meaning, while in reading intonation patterns are not present in the written material. Since a child speaks and sees *his* thoughts recorded, he can supply the correct intonation as he reads. The value of the language experience approach for teaching expression in oral reading should be acknowledged.

Characteristics of the Language Experience Approach

The characteristics of the language experience approach are implied in the definition, but for purposes of emphasis, three major characteristics are elaborated below.

Pupil-composed materials constitute a major source of reading materials in the language experience approach. Reading materials are developed as children talk about their ideas and experiences; their talk is recorded and the written record is then used for reading. In initial reading instruction, group and individual experience stories are used for reading instruction instead of published reading materials. Although pupil-produced materials are of prime importance, other materials are also utilized since children need to develop skill in reading and obtaining meaning from many types of materials. As children advance in skill, supplementary reading of selections from basal readers, trade books, newspapers, content area texts, and other materials is included in a well-rounded reading program. Chapters 3-9 devote considerable attention to the various types of and procedures for using pupil-developed reading materials.

The interrelationship of all the communication skills is stressed. Reading is not taught apart from but is dependent upon the other facets of the language arts. Reading is a language activity, and the ability to communicate through language is essential for success in reading. The four facets of the language arts can be classified as either receptive or expressive. Listening and reading are receptive while speaking and writing are

expressive. In the language experience approach, children's listening, speaking, and writing skills are incorporated with instruction in reading. As children increase their listening and speaking facility, they are increasing their ability to understand ideas encountered in thier reading.

There are no vocabulary controls in the reading materials other than the extent of a child's speaking vocabulary. The initial reading material is not limited to a few simple words or to short, artificial sentence patterns with a planned amount of repetition. There is, however, the inescapable repetition of frequently used words. In recording the pupil's speech, the teacher should *not* shorten or alter sentences in an attempt to control vocabulary. In the language experience approach when a pupil reads content which he has first spoken, the teacher is certain that the words employed in reading are in his speaking vocabulary. Ways of developing both speaking and reading vocabularies are discussed in Chapter 5.

Attributes of the Language Experience Approach

Definitions and characteristics provide one means of describing the language experience approach. However, teachers who work with this approach need a greater understanding of the philosophical framework or the distinctive attributes than that supplied by the definition and explanation given of the characteristics. The language experience approach is a personal, communicative, creative, and purposeful way of learning and teaching.

The language experience approach as a personal way of learning and teaching. The learner in the language experience approach is actively involved in the reading process as he creates and shares his reading. In the language experience approach it is possible to have material of high personal interest to each child. Group writing experiences are encouraged, but since the content of group stories will be related to common experiences and group interests, these materials will also be personal to the group members.

All teachers are confronted daily with the problem of creating an instructional program designed to reach individual interests and levels. Pupil-composed materials are one means of personalizing reading instruction. Robert Frost is reported to have said that the materials which help a good mind achieve the freedom essential for creativity are always different for each person.[5] The language experience approach uses different personal materials for each student.

The language experience approach as a communicative way of learning and teaching. In the language experience approach, reading occurs in a communication context and words are introduced, not in isolation, but in conjunction with a thought to be expressed. The child realizes that the printed words and sentences are a representation of an event or thought he already understands or has experienced. Dechant comments on the role of communication in reading: "Communication is the heart of the language arts. Without communication listening or reading cannot occur. Reading takes place only when the child shares the ideas that the communicator intends to convey."[6] In the language experience approach the child is communicating personally through the medium of print.

Communication requires effective use of language, and it is a goal of the language experience approach to develop children's language power by providing a rich language environment and the opportunity to articulate their thoughts. Allen refers to raising a child's level of sensitivity to his environment and heightening his awareness of language as a means

---

[5] Sidney Cox, *A Swinger of Birches: A Portrait of Robert Frost* (New York: Collier Books, 1961), p. 53.

[6] Dechant, *Improving the Teaching of Reading*, p. 87.

of expressing his knowledge of his world.[7] Directed language study starts with the present level of language development of the learner. In order to promote communication, the teacher must accept the language of the children and not block their speech through an emphasis on correction in the early stages of reading instruction.

The language experience approach as a creative way of learning and teaching. Creative thinking is an essential component in this approach to learning as children conceptualize thoughts and feelings through spoken and written language. Divergent responses are encouraged, accepted, and valued as children express themselves in the process of producing reading materials. Therefore, the child's role as a producer of personal materials for reading makes creative thinking a natural part of the learning act.

The teachers who seek to develop creativity realize that the classroom environment must be one which provides stimuli for and acceptance of creative thinking. The elementary school years are critical in the development of creative talent. Wilt comments on the teacher's role in freeing children to create: "First, you must believe that if a child is really to create something it must grow out of frequent opportunities to experiment and grope for his own best way to express his idea."[8] Teachers who use the language experience approach must believe that each child has some potential for creating and that he can express his creative efforts through the medium of language.

In classrooms where children's stories and language are accepted and valued, further expression is facilitated. A perfect final product is not the goal as much as is the *process* of creating and communicating through spoken and written language. The teacher has the responsibilty for providing the stimuli for creativity and must realize that in order to facilitate creating through language that children must have the opportunity to hear creative language models of others and to use language creatively in their own expression of ideas.

The language experience approach as a purposeful way of learning and teaching. The role of purpose in learning has been well established by learning theorists and educators. In the language experience approach, learning is purposeful when pupils feel a need to communicate through language activities. When a child has a personal stake in or purpose for

---

[7] R. Van Allen, *Attitudes and the Art of Teaching Reading* (Washington, D.C.: National Education Association, 1965), pp. 3-12.

[8] Miriam E. Wilt, *Creativity in the Elementary School* (New York: Appleton-Century-Crofts, 1959), p. 8.

learning to read, that purpose can have positive effects on his learning.

The language experience approach stresses the role of functional reading very early in the total reading program. Functional reading, which uses reading as a tool for learning as distinguished from learning the skills for how to read, constitutes one of the major aspects of a comprehensive reading program. In many school programs, functional reading does not receive much emphasis until the intermediate grades. However, functional reading is incorporated into the language experience approach in the beginning stages since the production of reading materials is often an outgrowth of classroom activities in content areas such as science and social studies. Reading activities should stem from significant class activities to maintain interest and motivation at a high level.

Attitudes for the Teacher in the Language Experience Approach

The teacher's interpretation of reading and of the processes of learning and teaching in relation to the individual influences the effectiveness of his teaching. In the language experience approach, the teacher *must* encourage freedom of expression in a setting in which creativity can flourish in order to promote growth in the ability to communicate.

Essential attitudes of the teacher in the language experience framework of teaching reading are:

1. The teacher must accept each child's language *as it is*, not as the teacher wishes it to be.

2. The teacher must recognize the creative nature of the language experience approach.

3. The teacher must recognize reading as a language activity which serves as a communication tool and must then integrate the teaching of reading and language.

In all language activities the teacher must accept the child's language as it is; he must not convey rejection by altering the language in order to have grammatically correct sentences which are not the actual recording of a child's speech. Allen states, ". . . , it is important to remember that each child has a natural language and that new language learnings must be related to it, faulty as it may be."[9] In our concern for developing language facility, we must be careful not to reject a child's existing level of communication skills. Facility in language skills will be fostered by opportunities for communicating personally valued ideas, not by a pro-

---

[9] Allen, *Attitudes and the Teaching of Reading*, p. 6.

gram of intensive correction. In the early stages correction of speech may serve to block oral and written expression rather than to encourage it. Lefevre warns:

> If teachers insist on instant correction, incessant correction, of every so-called mistake the child makes in speech, reading, and writing, the child will close up like an oyster. He will hate to recite and hate to write in school.[10]

Every child makes many mistakes in learning to talk but with opportunity and experience he develops the ability to communicate through speech. The process of communication is more important than the correctness of the mechanics. The preceding statements should (not imply that children are encouraged to learn incorrect speech patterns;) instead these statements emphasize that the first concern in the early stages of instruction is to develop the understanding that thoughts can be communicated orally and encoded with written symbols which then can be read with understanding. The teacher does have a responsibility to provide appropriate language models and to provide opportunities for expression so that communication skill does improve.

Acceptance is a key word for the teacher who recognizes the creative nature of the language experience approach. An attitude and climate of acceptance must be present if creativity is to flourish. Wilt comments on the importance of accepting a child's creative effort:

> The teacher should accept enthusiastically and generously whatever personal expression the child dreams up. Regardless of the creative result, he must always realize that the process is of far more consequence than the product.[11]

The language experience teacher will need to believe sincerely that children can be creative if teachers permit that creativity to be expressed and if they seek to reach it in a variety of ways. Teachers must believe in and develop pupil authorship.

Much has been stated in the preceding material concerning the stress on the interrelatedness of language and reading in the language experience approach. Acknowledgement of this concept is so important, however, that this third basic attitude of the teacher of recognition that reading and language should be taught as an integrated process is stressed again. The teacher has the responsibility for presenting situations which

---

[10] Lefevre, "Language and Self," *Elementary English*, XLIII, p. 128.
[11] Wilt, *Creativity in the Elementary School*, p. 8.

stimulate ever-increasing facility with language. The chasm which has often existed in elementary schools between the teaching of language and the teaching of reading is bridged in the language experience approach. Reading is viewed, not as a separate subject, but as a part of the language program. As children learn to communicate more effectively orally, they are learning to communicate more effectively through reading.

SUMMARY

The language experience approach uses children's oral language and experiences as the basis for creating personal reading materials. All of the communication skills are integrated in an instructional framework which stresses the personal, communicative, creative, and purposeful nature of this approach. The relationship of spoken and written language is emphasized when reading is taught with the language experience approach. Reading is viewed as a process of communication when oral language is represented by graphic symbols which are then decoded into speech sounds and the thoughts are associated with the reader's experience. The role of interest and personal involvement in learning is a major advantage of the language experience approach. Thinking is fostered as a child articulates his thoughts and produces his personal reading materials.

SUGGESTED READINGS

Ashton-Warner, Sylvia, *Teacher*. New York: Simon & Schuster, Inc., 1963. A personal account of Mrs. Ashton-Warner's experiences teaching Maori children in New Zealand, this book presents an inspiring philosophy of the language experience approach.

Lee, Dorris M. and R. V. Allen, *Learning to Read Through Experience*. New York: Appleton-Century-Crofts, 1963. Chapter 1. The first chapter of Lee and Allen's book stresses the interrelatedness of the communication skills and elaborates a child's concept of reading in a language-experience framework.

Shane, Harold G. *et al.*, *Improving Language Arts Instruction in the Elementary School*. Columbus: Charles E. Merrill Publishing Company, 1962. Chapter 1. The importance of communication in today's world is discussed in relation to the elementary language curriculum. The interrelationship of the expressive and receptive facets of language is elaborated. The beginning student of the language arts curriculum would find this a helpful background source.

Spache, George D. and Evelyn B. Spache, *Reading in the Elementary School.* New York: Allyn & Bacon, Inc., 1969. Chapter 6. The language experience approach is defined, and the advantages and limitations are discussed.

CHAPTER TWO

The Language Experience in the Total Reading Program

The language experience approach in the total reading program of the elementary school can be studied from several perspectives. In this chapter this approach is discussed as (1) an approach for initial reading instruction; (2) a supplement to other approaches beyond the beginning stages; (3) an approach for remedial readers; and (4) an approach for culturally disadvantaged children. Also included in this chapter is a discussion of this approach in relation to the goals of an elementary reading and language arts program. The remaining chapters contain specific suggestions for instruction related to these four classifications.

THE LANGUAGE EXPERIENCE APPROACH TO INITIAL READING INSTRUCTION

The major application of the language experience approach is as a way of teaching beginning reading. As a child first learns to read, he learns to recognize printed symbols and to associate the printed word forms with meanings built up through his previous experience. A child enters school with considerable competence in oral language, and instruction in reading should be integrally related to his existing speech development.

Before a child can comprehend the printed symbols of reading material, he must first be familiar with the oral language symbols which the printed words represent. The words a child encounters in beginning reading should be words which are already in his listening vocabulary. If the child has already learned the meaning of words he sees in print, he can relate the printed symbols to concepts already known.

In addition to stressing the relationship of reading to speaking, the language experience approach relates reading to writing and provides children with the opportunity to write extensively. The reports of the National First Grade Studies indicate that attention to writing experiences in conjunction with reading instruction is valuable. "There is evidence that a writing component is an effective addition to a primary reading program."[1] Hildreth explains the advantages of correlating reading instruction with writing in the following statements:

> Learning to read is reinforced by simultaneous experience in writing.

> In writing familiar language patterns, the young writer creates material to read expanding the amount of reading material that it is easy to understand because it reflects the child's own ideas, vocabulary, and modes of expression.

> Writing furnishes practice in using words in meaningful sentences, strengthening the association between word forms and their meaning, and the child's familiarity with sentence patterns.[2]

The beginning reading stage is a crucial one since later attitudes and achievement are influenced by a child's progress and reactions to the initial instruction. A child who experiences considerable frustration in beginning reading is very likely to develop a dislike of reading which will be a barrier to his progress at later stages. The role of success in learning to read is extremely important, and the language experience approach stresses success, as the beginning reader is able to read his dictated stories since he is certain of the content of these stories.

Many skills are involved in learning to read, and any approach to initial instruction must give attention to developing interest in reading, to building a reading vocabulary, to getting meaning from reading material, to developing skills for attacking unfamiliar words, and to teaching left-to-right progression across a line of print. In both the prereading and

---

[1] "National First Grade Studies," *The Reading Newsreport*, II (January, 1968), 41.
[2] Gertrude Hildreth, "Early Writing as an Aid to Reading," *Elementary English*, XL (January, 1963), 15, 18.

initial reading stages, attention also must be given to extending facility in oral language and to enriching the experience backgrounds since the ability to comprehend reading material is based on pupils' ability to understand oral language and on their experiences.

The language experience approach builds interest in reading through personal involvement and motivation in the creation of materials by the pupils. A sight vocabulary is built, not through reading basal textbooks, but by learning to recognize words used in individual and class stories. Comprehension is present since the content was meaningful when first expressed through speech. Some instruction in word attack skills is begun as pupils notice the beginnings and endings of words and as they analyze some of the words in their word banks (see Chapters 5 and 8) for similar phonetic elements. Children's attention is called to left-to-right progression in reading as the teacher reads the group experience stories aloud and as she helps children read their individual stories.

In initial reading instruction, the materials in the language experience approach are chiefly pupil-composed and based on pupils' language and experience. These pupil-composed materials include both group and individual experience stories, and both group and individual word banks. A group experience story is a record of some common experience or topic of interest which is discussed by the pupils and is written by the teacher. A personal story is dictated to the teacher who records or types it for the child to use as his reading material. Individual word banks are built as a child can identify words in the group experience stories and in his own stories. Words are written on separate cards or slips of paper to be kept by each child for his word bank. These banks can tell the teacher which words are in the child's sight vocabulary and can be used as examples for instruction in phonics. Group word banks can be compiled as the class studies different classifications of words. For example, there could be categories of animal words, color words, descriptive words, action words, and others.

A writing center is an important part of the classroom environment, and children's literature is a part of the total reading program. The writing center functions as a stimulus for independent creative writing and for following up language study as materials and ideas for creating stories are displayed. (Detailed description of procedures for using the above types of materials is given in Chapters 3-9.)

Instruction in reading is started by having a child dictate a story or by writing a group experience story with the total class. However, in the early stages of instruction, it should be remembered that such instruction will have different emphases and values for different children. With the first stories some children will learn to read some words. Other children will be able to recognize likenesses and differences in printed words and letters but will not be able to read individual words immediately. For some children the most important contribution the early stories can offer is helping them to see that their spoken ideas can be put into written form. Other children may profit most from the oral discussion which precedes the writing of the story. For all children the meaning of the written record should be clear.

When used as the major approach to beginning reading, the language experience approach can be used without instructional textbooks until pupils are reading at a first reader level. At this level of reading development, the language experience approach is used as a supplement to or in combination with reading textbooks or in a program of individualized reading in trade books. The combined approach is discussed in the next section.

When achievement scores in reading were compared in a study of the basal reader, individualized, and language experience approaches in San Diego County, California, the language experience approach was found to be as effective as the other two approaches in the primary grades.[3] In the National First Grade Studies, the language experience approach was found to be an effective means of teaching beginning reading.[4] Hahn reported that the time provided for purposeful writing, speaking, and listening in conjunction with wide reading contributed to the reading achievement of pupils using the language experience approach.[5]

THE LANGUAGE EXPERIENCE APPROACH IN COMBINATION WITH OTHER APPROACHES

In the total elementary reading program, the language experience approach has many advantages when employed in combination with other approaches. While teachers may not want to rely on the language experience approach as the major means of reading instruction beyond the beginning stages, they will want to incorporate many of its aspects. The high degree of personal involvement and the functional application of reading, speaking, listening, and writing are features which strongly support the use of language experience beyond the initial reading stage. In fact, the activities suggested in Chapters 3-9 can be easily incorporated into the language experience framework as a corollary to other approaches.

A number of authorities have commented on the value of an enriched reading program which combines features of various approaches. One of the major findings of the National First Grade Studies was that any approach which is enriched with features of other approaches produces better reading achievement than the use of one approach exclusively.[6] Stauffer and Hammond reported that the language experience approach which was effective in grade one continued to be effective at the second grade level.[7] They found that the pupils taught with the language experience approach developed greater facility in written communication than did those taught with the basal reader approach. Kendrick and Bennett also found the language experience approach to be effective through the

---

[3] R. Van Allen, "More Ways Than One," *Childhood Education*, XXXVIII (November, 1961), 108-111.

[4] Guy L. Bond and Robert Dykstra, "The Cooperative Research Program in First-Grade Reading Instruction," *Reading Research Quarterly*, II (Summer, 1967).

[5] Harry T. Hahn, "Three Approaches to Beginning Reading Instruction—ITA, Language Experience and Basic Readers—Extended to Second Grade," *The Reading Teacher*, XX (May, 1967), p. 715.

[6] Bond and Dykstra, "Cooperative Research Program."

[7] Russell G. Stauffer and W. Dorsey Hammond, "The Effectiveness of Language Arts and Basic Reader Approaches to First Grade Reading Instruction," *The Reading Teacher*, XX (May, 1967), 740-746.

second grade.[8] Vilsek, Cleland, and Bilka noted that pupils taught with the language experience approach through the second grade could demonstrate superiority in comprehension of concepts and in reading in the content areas of science, social studies, and arithmetic. They felt that the diversity of reading diets probably contributed to this superiority.[9]

As children move beyond the initial stages of instruction, personally created reading materials have serious limitations for providing a complete reading program. Exposure to other types of reading materials must be provided. Many of the enrichment suggestions in manuals of basal readers could be combined with the ideas of the following chapters. The basal reading program can provide a systematic development of reading skills while the language experience activities can add personal involvement and application of language skills.

Individualized reading which features the wide reading of library materials, pupil-teacher conferences, and self-selection can be combined with language experience activities. Some teachers who use the language experience approach in beginning reading move into an individualized program when children have acquired a sufficiently large sight vocabulary to read simple library books. The pupil-teacher conference is featured in the language experience method with the individual experience stories and in individualized reading discussons. Flexible grouping in the individualized program allows for formation of interest groups as children talk about their independent reading and as they share their personal stories with each other. The suggestions for working with literature in Chapter 6 will be helpful in combining independent individualized reading with language experiences activities.

The three major characteristics of pupil-composed materials, lack of a controlled vocabulary, and integration of all the language arts still are basic when the language experience approach is combined with other approaches. Emphasis is placed on developing facility in written language, on enriching the speaking and writing vocabularies as well as the reading vocabulary, and on providing integration of reading skills with other facets of communication at the higher levels. The personal, communicative, creative, and purposeful attributes of the language experience approach also operate when this approach is used in combination with other approaches and materials. In a combined program the pupil-

---

[8] William M. Kendrick and Clayton L. Bennett, "A Comparative Study of Two First Grade Language Arts Programs—Extended into Second Grade," *The Reading Teacher*, XX (May, 1967), 747-755.

[9] Elaine C. Vilsek, Donald L. Clelend, and Loisanne Bilka, "Coordinating and Integrating Language Arts Instruction," *The Reading Teacher*, XXI (October, 1967), p. 10.

composed materials are not used as much for reading as for stimulating creative expression, for developing power in communicating in spoken and written language, and for providing motivation for using the skills of written expression.

THE LANGUAGE EXPERIENCE APPROACH
FOR REMEDIAL READERS

The language experience approach has merit for remedial readers who have experienced frustration in reading with conventional or traditional approaches. Children with reading problems often exhibit a negative attitude toward reading and may reject remediation attempts which may be more of the same type of instruction which was unsuccessful in the past. Attitude, success, and motivation are of primary importance in working with remedial readers. For pupils who possess a negative attitude toward reading as a result of repeated frustration and failure, the use of personal stories can remove the fear of failure. The language experience approach promotes a favorable attitude toward reading and develops a high degree of personal involvement with intrinsic motivation as students experience success through the reading of their experience stories.

Johnson states five fundamental principles of learning which underlie working with remedial readers:

1. Learning begins with the known.
2. Learning proceeds from concrete to abstract.
3. Learning demands active participation.
4. Learning should be goal directed.
5. Learning is an individual matter.[10]

The language experience approach does begin with known material which is easily decoded and understood, does provide concrete materials as the starting point, does actively involve the learner, does help the learner to be goal-directed, and does approach reading in an individual manner with concern for a personal involvement in the reading situation. The descriptions of the language experience approach and the techniques described in Chapters 3-8 can be adapted for remedial reading in-

---

[10] Marjorie S. Johnson, "Basic Considerations in Corrective Instruction," in *Corrective Reading in the Classroom, Perspectives in Reading No. 7*, eds. Marjorie S. Johnson and Roy A. Kress (Newark, Delaware: International Reading Association, 1966), pp. 64-68.

struction. The basic idea of starting with the pupil's language to create reading materials is again followed when this approach is used with remedial readers. Using the spoken language of the reader is an advantage since the remedial student has usually advanced in oral language beyond the language of the textbooks on his instructional level. For example, the fifth grade child who is reading on a first grade reading level will be more advanced in his oral language than the language employed in a first grade reader, and he will have little interest in the content of the easy book designed for a child of six.

After the student has experienced some success through personal experience stories, he can move on to other materials or the language experience procedures can be integrated with a combined approach. As he works with experience stories, needed work in skills can be provided by studying words used in his stories which illustrate the particular word attack generalization to be mastered. Comprehension skills can also be developed through the personal experience stories, especially for those students who "word-call" instead of reading with meaning.

The author acknowledges the need for careful evaluation of each remedial reader's strengths and weaknesses and realizes that the instructional approach selected must be adapted to the particular reading needs of each student. Specific skill deficiencies must be diagnosed and appropriate instruction offered. The language experience approach is not suggested as a panacea for all remedial cases, but is recommended as one approach which may help some children with reading difficulties, especially from the standpoint of developing favorable attitudes and for illustrating the relationship between oral and written language.

THE LANGUAGE EXPERIENCE APPROACH FOR THE CULTURALLY DISADVANTAGED

Culturally disadvantaged children experience considerable difficulty and frustration with traditional methods of reading instruction. As a result of reading problems, these children are handicapped in all school activities which require reading. The language experience approach for disadvantaged children is of greatest relevance in the beginning stages of instruction; however, it continues to be important for teaching communication skills at higher levels.

Factors involved in the difficulties disadvantaged children experience in reading and other language learning include: lack of readiness for school, limited experiential backgrounds, meager opportunity for oral language development in the pre-school years, poor self-concept, a negative attitude toward school, and culturally foreign curriculum materials and programs. It is well known that the disadvantaged child is particularly deficient in language skills and that the majority of school materials are not related to either his language patterns or vocabulary. Ravitz comments on the unreality of reading textbooks for disadvantaged children:

> A curious social psychological obstacle confronting the children of depressed areas is the unreality of the textbook world they are expected to explore and understand. The usual textbooks are those that draw their characters, their language patterns, their attitudes and their values from the world of the white middle class. Such a world is an unreal one for most residents of depressed areas. It is a world beyond their experience and they falter in it.[11]

Developing skills of thinking, listening, speaking, writing, and reading along with a feeling of personal worth and self-confidence are major concerns in school programs for disadvantaged children. The language experience approach has particular merit for disadvantaged pupils since the focus is on oral language as the basis for reading and on developing the ability to communicate through language which is so desperately needed. If the language experience approach is employed with the disadvantaged, the reading materials will be in their language patterns, and these children can be given the much needed opportunity to talk about their experiences.

Of crucial importance is the acceptance of the disadvantaged child's existing language as reading materials are developed. The intent is to use his present level of language development as the medium of communication through which he learns to read. For example, the following story was dictated by a child in a city slum:

> Her is Mom.
> Her braids my hair.
> Her cleans around.
> Her shouts me to watch Eddie.
> Nothing else.[12]

For this child to have her story recorded using "she" for "her" in the first two sentences would probably result in her reading the printed word

---

[11] Mel Ravitz, "The Role of the School in Urban Settings," in *Education in Depressed Areas*, A. Harry Passow, ed. (New York: Bureau of Publications, Teachers College, Columbia University, 1963), p. 17.

[12] "Poignant Drawings are Helping Slum Children Learn to Read," *The Washington Post*, August 28, 1966, Sec. F., p. 13.

"she" as "her" thus resulting in confusion of word forms. If the pronoun "she" is not in her oral language background, it should not *at this stage* be used in the reading material.

The need for realistic reading programs which offer maximum opportunity to develop the culturally disadvantaged child's ability to communicate is pressing. The language experience approach which employs reading materials based on pupils' experiences and expressed in their language patterns is one means of providing meaningful reading content. A moving compilation of writings of ghetto children is found in *The Me Nobody Knows* edited by Stephen M. Joseph.[13] In *Hooked on Books* by Daniel Fader,[14] personal writing was one feature of a program developed to reach disadvantaged and delinquent youth through exposure to paperback books. The examples included in these two sources show dramatically the relevancy and impact of personal writing for the disadvantaged.

Stauffer and Cramer report, "When, . . . , the disadvantaged person is given an opportunity to read accounts that he has produced, which reflect his thinking about things important to him, and which are a part of his direct experience, his progress is often dramatic."[15] The language experience approach can be an intensive effort to compensate for and to alleviate the major problems of a lack of readiness for reading, the inappropriate story content of reading textbooks, and the oral language difficulties which handicap culturally disadvantaged children in reading. Through stimulating experiences and intense personal involvement, the language experience approach can introduce reading to disadvantaged children in a personal, communicative, creative, and purposeful manner.

THE GOALS OF THE LANGUAGE EXPERIENCE APPROACH

A program of reading instruction in the elementary school must have clearly stated goals for the pupils involved. If reading is defined as a process of decoding print, the instructional approach selected will stress decoding; if reading is defined as a thinking process, the instructional approach used will concentrate on the development of thinking skills in

---

[13] Stephen M. Joseph, ed., *The Me Nobody Knows* (New York: Avon Books, 1969).

[14] Daniel N. Fader, *Hooked on Books: Program and Proof* (New York: Berkley Publishing Corporation, 1968).

[15] Russell G. Stauffer and Ronald L. Cramer, "Reading Specialists in an Occupational Training Program," *The Reading Teacher*, XX (March, 1967), p. 528.

reading. In Chapter 1 reading was defined as a communication skill which includes the decoding of print and the association of meaning with the decoded printed symbols. As a child matures in his reading development, the decoding of print can be emphasized to a lesser degree, and greater emphasis can be placed on higher levels of thinking.

The primary goal of reading instruction is to develop children's ability to use reading as a medium of communication. The language experience approach must, like any approach to reading instruction, build children's reading vocabularies, establish effective means of word attack, develop comprehension ability, and promote a favorable attitude toward and permanent interest in reading. Applegate identifies the goals of the language arts as follows:

> To use words responsibly
> To think clearly
> To listen imaginatively
> To speak effectively
> To read thoughtfully
> To write creatively
> To use mechanics powerfully
> To regard good English respectfully
> To acquaint children with the best (literature)[16]

The preceding goals apply to a broad interpretation of the language experience approach and emphasize the significance and interrelatedness of all the language arts in this approach to reading. A successful language experience reading program teaches both reading and language arts skills in situations which necessitate meaningful communication.

SUMMARY

The language experience approach is employed for initial reading instruction, for remedial readers, for culturally disadvantaged children, and as a supplement to other approaches. The teacher must accept the children's existing level of language development and their language patterns as they create their personal reading materials. The primary goal of reading and language arts instruction in the language experience framework is to develop the ability to communicate in all facets of language. The

---

[16] Mauree Applegate, *Easy in English* (Evanston, Illinois: Row, Peterson and Company, 1962), p. 8.

goals of developing word attack skills, wide reading vocabulary, comprehension, and a permanent interest in reading must also be included in the language experience approach.

SUGGESTED READING

Allen, R. Van., *Attitudes and the Art of Teaching Reading.* Washington, D.C.: National Education Association, 1965. This pamphlet includes background information for the teacher as well as classroom profiles of kindergarten, primary, and remedial reading classes.

Black, Millard, "Programs for the Culturally Disadvantaged," in *First Grade Reading Programs, Perspectives in Reading No. 5,* ed. James A. Kerfoot. Newark, Delaware: International Reading Association, 1965, pp. 150-72. The description of reading programs for disadvantaged children includes a description of language experience programs being used with disadvantaged children.

Kohl, Herbert A., *Teaching the "Unteachable".* New York: The New York Review, 1967. Kohl includes many examples of the writings of disadvantaged children to illustrate that children can write creatively and expressively when provided the freedom and encouragement to do so without the drudgery and dislike frequently associated with English composition.

Stauffer, Russell G., "A Language Experience Approach," in *First Grade Reading Programs, Perspectives in Reading No. 5,* ed. James A. Kerfoot. Newark, Delaware: International Reading Association, 1965, pp. 86-118. Procedures for the language experience approach in beginning reading instruction are described in detail. Emphasis is on pupil-composed materials such as individual and group experience stories and word banks.

Wilson, Robert M., *Diagnostic and Remedial Reading for Classroom and Clinic.* Columbus, Ohio: Charles E. Merrill Publishing Company, 1967. The topics of diagnosis and remediation are the major emphasis of this informative source on working with problem readers.

CHAPTER THREE

Experience Stories

One of the major types of reading material in the language experience approach is the experience story. These can be either individual or group stories; both are widely used. A variation of the group experience story is the group book which is composed from separate pages by different children about a selected topic. In this chapter individual experience stories, group experience stories, and group books are discussed with emphasis upon the procedures for developing and using them in the teaching of reading and language skills.

The *process* of developing and using the story is the most important consideration, not the final product or the form of the story itself. The familiarization with the procedures should free the teacher to concentrate on the *communication* process in the *formulation* of the content, in the *recording* of the story, and in the *reading experiences* connected with the story. Tiedt and Tiedt define writing as "thought transferred to paper."[1] Encouraging thinking is essential in the process of creating experience stories if children are to view the writing process as the use of letter symbols to record thoughts. Ideas, not mechanics of writing, should be the major concern.

---

[1] Iris M. Tiedt and Sidney W. Tiedt, *Contemporary English in the Elementary School* (Englewood Cliffs, N. J.: Prentice-Hall, Inc., 1967), p. 145.

In this chapter many of the comments for using experience stories apply to the beginning stages of reading instruction, but adaptations can be made for higher levels. The development of experience stories at any level follows the sequence of having children express thoughts through speaking, the recording of these thoughts in printed language, and finally the reading of the story, with emphasis on communication in each of the three steps.

As children mature in language skills and as the number of words they are able to write independently increases, the experience story becomes less teacher-directed and more pupil-directed. The focus changes from complete dependence upon the teacher as recorder to limited teacher assistance and finally to independent creative writing. Even though the level of material and difficulty of content increases, the values of personal authorship remain. At higher levels, the written story is used less for teaching reading skills and vocabulary and is used more for furthering creative expression through written language. In Chapter 4 creative writing in the language experience approach is described in detail.

As reading materials for initial instruction in reading, experience stories have the following advantages:

1. Experience stories permit the introduction of reading skills in a meaningful situation since the materials are written in the children's language using their sentence patterns and vocabulary.
2. Experience stories provide a gradual and natural transition from the pre-reading stage to the stage of beginning reading.
3. The material is easily comprehended since it is a record of children's thoughts.
4. Experience stories can promote success and favorable attitudes in the beginning stages since no pressure is exerted for mastery of a given number of words.
5. Experience stories demonstrate the relationship between spoken and written language. Children *see* that their speech can be recorded with print.
6. Experience stories involve the learner personally.

These stories can contribute to the development of reading and language skills in several ways. Children develop a basic reading vocabulary as they learn to identify words in their stories. They realize that reading is a process of associating meaning with printed words. Experience stories can be used to demonstrate left-to-right sequence in a realistic reading situation. Growth in oral language is fostered as the teacher develops awareness of words through provision of situations for speaking and listening. The organization of ideas in a logical sequence can be developed through the practice of creating experience stories. The feeling of personal accomplishment which comes from being the producer of reading material is an important contribution. The feeling of self-confidence that comes from being able to read his own stories affects a child's attitude toward reading.

GROUP EXPERIENCE STORIES

In the development of a group experience story the children participate in an event or discussion of an an event or selected topic. The children's ideas are recorded and then used for reading material. The teacher must give consideration to motivation, oral discussion of the experience, recording, reading, and follow-up activities.

During the discussion a number of pupils contribute ideas and a group chart is made representing the various thinking. Although the number of children involved may not be large, the teacher can provide opportunities for all pupils to participate in this type of activity since he will be working with chart stories frequently.

The subject of a group story should be something familiar. The teacher has the responsibility for providing motivating experiences which are appropriate and worthwhile, however, many opportunities for using charts will occur in every classroom. Lists of classroom duties, charts of standards, letters to other classes, letters relating to field trips, and weather records present excellent opportunities for charts in functional situations. However, the majority of the group experience stories will be of the narrative type which the children compose creatively. Trips, pets, classroom events, pictures, classroom interest centers, and unit activities provide ever-changing stimuli for group experience stories. Materials which are available commercially can be used to stimulate language experience stories. *The Visual Lingual Reading Program* of 48 color transparencies from Tweedy Transparencies,[2] the pictures of the *Ginn Kit A*,[3] the *Peabody Language Development Kits*,[4] and the *Picture Portfolio Pictures to Read* of the Chandler Publishing Company[5] are particularly helpful.

---

[2] M. Jerry Weiss, ed. *et al.*, *The Visual Lingual Reading Program*, Series 1710 (East Orange, N.J.: Tweedy Transparencies, 1967).

[3] Theodore Clymer, Bernice Christenson, and David Russell, *Kit A* (Boston: Ginn and Company, 1965).

[4] Lloyd M. Dunn and James O. Smith, *Peabody Language Development Kits*, Levels I, II, III (Minneapolis: American Guidance Service, 1965, 1966, 1967).

[5] *Picture Portfolio Pictures to Read*, Chandler Reading Readiness Program (San Francisco: Chandler Publishing Co., 1965).

The group discussion which precedes the writing of the children's ideas provides an important language activity. The discussion experience gives children the opportunity to express and hear ideas in oral language. In discussion situations habits of listening can be established and the teacher can observe and evaluate the language facility of the children. It must be remembered, too, that extending both the experience and language backgrounds of children is a prime concern in the language arts instruction.

The teacher records the pupils' ideas on the chalkboard or on chart paper *using the language of the pupils.* These stories should reflect the oral language patterns of the group composing them, not the teacher's polishing of their language to meet his standards of "good" English. If desired, a title is selected by the children and then used in the written record. Appropriate punctuation and capitalization are used as needed. Manuscript writing is used with large letters for easy visibility with careful spacing between words so that the beginning reader can see the relationship of one written word for each spoken word. No attempt is made to control the vocabulary or to limit sentence length.

The first reading of a group experience story is usually done by the teacher immediately after the recording. In the initial stages of reading instruction, the teacher will emphasize the left-to-right progression across a line of print as she reads the story to the group. Then, she may ask the group to read the story with her. Then, a few children will read the story with as much help as necessary. If the original recording was done on the chalkboard, the teacher will copy the story on primary chart paper with a felt-tip pen. Children may be asked to illustrate the chart. Additional reading of the chart will be done on following days with some of the activities suggested below.

The following story was dictated by a first grade class during the first week of school.

The Rabbit's Nature

He eats carrots and cabbage.
He's lonesome when his mother is away.
He doesn't go anywhere.
He looks black.

The title was a surprise to the teacher but when the child who suggested it was asked why he wanted that title, he replied, "Well, the story tells what the rabbit is like!" The story was recorded with the children's language exactly as they said it. The contractions were used since they were a part of the children's speech. No attempt was made to repeat or change vocabulary.

In the first step the group talked about the small black rabbit which the teacher had brought to school. In the second step the teacher recorded the children's ideas. Next the teacher read the story to the group, and then the children read the story with her. Individual copies were made for each child and were used for the follow-up activities.

A completed experience record is displayed in the classroom and is used again for various reading activities. In most cases, three or four days will be the maximum spent with any one chart. It is preferable to write and read many charts rather than to over-drill on a few. The group experience stories may be collected on a chart rack for reference in the following weeks. The teacher may type or print the stories for compilation in a class book which will be available in the class library or on the reading table, or he may duplicate copies of the stories for each child to keep in an individual book. The duplicated copy of a group experience story may be taken home by the child to share with his parents. Word, phrase, and sentence cards which correspond with words on the chart can be made, and children can match the cards to the content of the chart. Children can also work independently with matching words and phrases if they are given two duplicated copies and are asked to cut out individual words to match to words in the intact copy. For children who have not yet begun to read, the group chart can be used to provide practice in letter recognition. Children can match letter cards to letters on the chart and can name letters in the experience story.

The stories can also be used in the development of class or individual word banks as pupils identify words of various categories. (See page 63). For example, a chart about the leaves in the fall could be used to start a classification of color words. "Animal" words, "action" words, "naming" words, and other categories also would evolve from the experience stories. If a child can read a word or words in a group story, those words can be added to his individual word bank.

Stauffer suggests dividing a first grade class into groups and developing experience stories with each. The pace of the instruction and the extent of follow-up activities will vary depending upon the ability of the group.[6]

The group experience story approach can be adapted for teaching manuscript writing in grade one. The teacher will need to explain that what they write will be much shorter than a chart story but that they can write their own ideas. There will be oral discussion of an experience or idea, determining the example the children want to record. For instance, the rabbit story on p. 29 could serve as the stimulus with a short sentence such as "The rabbit hops" or "The rabbit is black" selected for the writing activity. The teacher will demonstrate on a chalkboard, large writing paper, or a transparency for the overhead projector, the formation of each letter as the children reproduce the letters for their individual papers. After the writing, the sentence is read so that children feel that their writing communicates an idea. In the stages of first learning to write, the sentence will probably consist of only three or four words. As skill in writing develops, the length of sentences and the stories will increase.

Although group charts may not be as widely used after the first half of grade one, some children are still operating at the pre-reading and initial stages of reading well into grade one and beyond. For these students, the group experience stories are particularly valuable. Most children, however, will have progressed to a combined approach using language experience materials along with basal readers and library books. Beyond the beginning stages of reading, the group chart serves as a functional language activity and is a record of important events within the class.

Edwards describes the following five-step procedure for using the language experience approach in a group situation with remedial students

---

[6] Russell G. Stauffer, "The Language Experience Approach," in *First Grade Reading Programs, Perspectives in Reading No. 5*, ed. James A. Kerfoot (Newark, Delaware: International Reading Association, 1965), pp. 93-102.

who were either disadvantaged adolescents or functionally illiterate adults. 1. The teacher stimulates and guides a discussion of a topic or experience. 2. The group's ideas are recorded (by one or all members). 3. Logical sentences and paragraphs are constructed from the randomly recorded thoughts. 4. There is silent reading of the entire selection after it has been duplicated for all students. 5. A variety of follow-up activities can be conducted by small groups or individual students.[7] The teaching of vocabulary, pronunciation, comprehension, and word attack skills is incorporated as needed in the above sequence especially at steps three and five.

INDIVIDUAL EXPERIENCE STORIES

The concept that his speech can be put into written form is a key one for a child using the language experience approach and is best developed through the personal experience story. Personal stories have the same advantages of the group stories and, in addition, probably stimulate more interest in reading because of the greater personal involvement.

Often children are familiar with the procedures for developing a group story before they compose individual stories. Therefore, they are familiar with the practice of talking about an experience or idea and seeing the thoughts encoded into written symbols which they can then read. As was true for group stories, in using individual stories the teacher must consider motivation, oral discussion, recording and reading of the stories, and follow-up activities.

Often the motivation for individual stories is conducted with the total class or with a sub-group as the teacher presents an idea, topic, or picture as the stimulus for discussion. Oral language discussions preceding the development of individual stories are necessary to promote the language development of some pupils and to encourage thinking. Through questioning, the teacher seeks to elicit pupil interest and response. She may use a picture or object to ask: "What do you see?" "What does this make you think of?" "What happened first?" "What happened next?" "What would you like to do?" Trips, pictures, individual experiences, events, literature, art work, birthdays, pets, and special interests can provide the stimulus for an individual story.

These stories are usually recorded in manuscript writing or with a primary typewriter. Teachers may choose the form easier for them while recognizing that the young reader may prefer the typewritten form since

---

[7] Thomas J. Edwards, "The Language Experience Approach on Cultural Deprivation," *The Reading Teacher*, XVIII (April, 1965), pp. 546-551.

it is more like the print in books. The recorded story should be in such a form as to create pride in its author. A uniform size is desirable if pupil folders of class books are to be compiled with the various stories. In some schools teacher aides or upper grade children are available to record children's dictated stories.

Immediately after the recording of an individual story, the teacher reads the story to the child. (After the beginning stages of instruction, reading by the teacher can be omitted.) The teacher and child read the story together, and then the pupil can read it alone with teacher help where needed. The next step is for the teacher to ask the child to identify the words he can read in the story. As the child says he knows a particular word, it is written on a card for his word bank.

After children have a basic sight vocabulary, the teacher does not have to hear all the reading of all stories written by the pupils. As the language experience approach is used in connection with other approaches beyond the beginning stages, the children will read many materials in addition to the personal stories. At this time the personal stories become more important as an outlet for creative expression rather than as a means of teaching initial reading. The creative stories can be shared in small group settings so that children have an opportunity for oral reading and for hearing the creative work of their peers.

After the stories have been recorded and read with the teacher, the child is ready to work independently with his story. The types of activity which follow the reading depend upon the child's stage of development. In the beginning stages of reading, he can underline or circle those words which he can identify or which he had identified with the teacher during the first reading session. The words he can read will become part of his word bank. He can take the word cards from his bank and use them for visual discrimination practice and for practice in word recognition as he matches the words in his bank to words in his story. At later stages of development, the reader can identify the words he does *not* know. The latter procedure is followed only after he can recognize all but a few of the words in the story.

Illustrating stories is a popular activity for children and adds to the appeal of the finished product. In fact, pupil illustrations provide one of the strongest impetuses for producing personal materials. It is the illustrations, too, as well as the thoughts expressed, which contribute to the individuality of the stories. Often personal experience stories will originate from illustrations. Pictures can serve as the stimulus for creating a story. Teachers may find that for pupils who are reluctant to create stories that having them tell a story about their pictures is the easiest way to begin pupil authorship.

In an experimental project in the District of Columbia, Poloroid cameras were made available for teachers. The personal response to pictures of themselves triggered story production from some children who had not reacted to any other stimulus.

Often the teacher may want to display children's illustrated stories with appropriate captions on bulletin boards. A feeling of pride and achievement results when a child realizes that his story is valued enough to be used for classroom display. The bulletin board displays can stimulate children to read their stories to their classmates, thereby providing additional reading practice.

After individual stories are written, pupils can keep them in a folder. Some teachers make carbon copies when typing the stories for the children for evaluation of the child's progress or for display.

When the children have written and read the individual stories the teacher may form small groups for the purpose of sharing the stories. Oral reading expression can be stressed in this audience type situation, and personal accomplishment will be felt. The teacher is available to help with difficult words so that no child is placed in a situation where he will be unsuccessful. Listening habits are practiced in a functional situation. Children can tape their stories, and the recordings can be used in the listening center.

Individual stories can be placed in the reading corner for independent reading by the rest of the class. Occasionally, the stories can be shown with an opaque projector for reading. The teacher can invite children from another class to hear a group of children read their stories. Occasionally the stories are collected for a class book. The library shelves in the class can include a section of children's stories. In some schools, children's original stories have been placed in the school's central library collection. The motivation of the above practices is obvious.

Chapters 4 and 6 also contain suggestions for stimulating the writing of individual stories.

GROUP BOOKS

Another popular type of pupil-developed reading material is the group book which is produced by combining the efforts of a number of pupils. Usually the group books are comprised of collections of pages on the same topic by different children. At higher levels as the group books are related to content in social studies and science, each page may deal with a different aspect of an identified topic. Some group books may be written as follow-ups to children's literature materials. Some may be collections of children's creative stories. Others will develop from class discussions, while still others will be outgrowths of study in other curriculum areas. Group books are an excellent source of pupil-composed material for the classroom reading corner.

Since group books are cooperative efforts, the motivation and preliminary discussion of the content will ordinarily be in a group setting. In the beginning stages of reading instruction, group books may consist of one sentence with an illustration for each page. For example, one first grade teacher was discussing the color red and had the children draw a picture and dictate a sentence about something which was red. The book had a red construction paper cover and was called, "Red Things." Some sentences were, "The sun at night is red," "My dress is red," and "A crayon is red." At a more advanced level the books can contain more involved content about more advanced topics and are often written as committee projects related to content areas. These books can be a means of functional writing and reading when pupils use them for recording information and for reporting information to their classmates. For example, if the class had been studying a science unit on electricity, a group book on this topic could be written with each child reporting different information pertinent to the unit.

As children illustrate their respective pages, the teacher can record the accompanying sentences as she circulates among the group. For reasons of motivation, each child's page or contribution should be labeled with his name. The books can be easily assembled by using loose-leaf metal rings. The teacher will read the finished book to the class and may ask each child to read his page. After the books are completed, they should be displayed on the library table for independent reading and for children to examine during their free time. Word cards from the group books should be made available on the same table where the books are displayed. Copies of the books can be duplicated for each child. Some group books may be donated to the school library. The group books can be used for word study as children select words to be added to the class word bank(s) and as individual children identify known words to be added to their personal banks.

For children who are having difficulty with reading in the content areas of science and social studies, the language procedures for pupil-composed materials can be particularly useful. For example, with a particular topic, the teacher could provide the stimulus for learning by a field trip, pictures, a film strip, or by conducting an experiment. The next step would be oral discussion of the experiences and content. Pupils' ideas are recorded and the content is then in their language and is available as reading material. As additional experiences occur, more pupil-

composed material will be developed. In effect, pupils are creating their own texts.

In motivating experience stories with children of limited experience backgrounds, a teacher may direct the discussion more specifically and may narrow the topic considerably. For example, the simple question which relates to something very concrete and personal within the realm of children's experiences can be used. Questions such as the following could be asked:

> What is your name?
> What things are green (red, yellow, etc.)?
> Where do you live?
> Who is your friend?
> What do you like to do?
> Who is in your family?
> How old are you?
> What do you like to eat?
> What color is your shirt?
> What did you see on your way to school?

Many additional questions of this nature could be posed, and in many cases, a one sentence answer could constitute the entire individual story in the beginning stages. In using this technique, the teacher must be careful not to limit children's talking to this type of expression but should realize that this technique can be a way of starting to put children's speech into written form.

Personal stories, bulletin board displays, group books, and group charts could be developed in connection with each of the topics suggested previously.

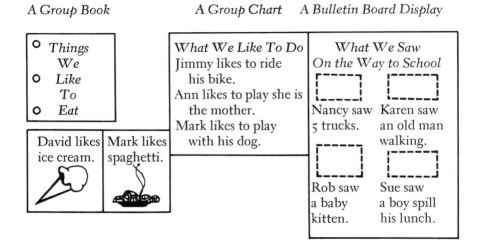

| *A Group Book* | *A Group Chart* | *A Bulletin Board Display* |

SUMMARY

Group experience stories, individual experience stories, and group books are the major types of pupil-composed materials in the language experience approach. The procedures for developing these three types of materials are similar since attention is given to motivation, discussion, recording, reading, and follow-up activities in each. The motivation and oral discussion which precede the recording of pupils' thoughts are stressed, and the recording is in their language. Reading of the material occurs immediately after its creation, and follow-up activities are provided for extra practice and direct teaching of skills. The focus is on the acceptance of the children's language and on functional and creative aspects of the experience stories in the total classroom program.

SUGGESTED READINGS

Herrick, Virgil E. and Marcella Nerbovig, *Using Experience Charts with Children*. Columbus: Charles E. Merrill Publishing Company, 1964. Detailed instructions for constructing and using experience charts with children are described. The illustrations depicting examples make this a valuable resource for the teacher who is learning how to use experience charts. Many types are discussed with application to various curriculum areas and grade levels.

Lee, Dorris M. and R. V. Allen, *Learning to Read Through Experience*. New York: Appleton-Century-Crofts, 1963, pp. 30-73. Lee and Allen describe both the types and uses of experience charts as they explain the place of experience stories in the framework of language experiences in reading.

Stauffer, Russell G., "The Language Experience Approach," in *First Grade Reading Programs, Perspectives in Reading No. 5*, ed. James A. Kerfoot. Newark, Delaware: International Reading Association, 1965, pp. 86-118. Stauffer discusses the use of group experience stories in beginning reading instruction in first grade. With a specific example he describes the motivation, oral discussion, recording, reading, and follow-up activities in detail.

CHAPTER FOUR

Writing Creatively in the Language Experience Approach

Developing pupil authorship is a major concern of the language experience approach. Other language experiences feed into the process of creating through written expression. A basic principle of the language experience approach is that pupils *can* create materials for reading. The pupil-composed materials of the language experience approach provide a natural impetus for creative writing. As children transform their thoughts into written form through the encoding of their speech, and as they read their stories, they are integrating all the communication skills.

Creative writing springs from personal experiences which pupils wish to communicate through written language. In creative writing, responses must be personal and must come from the pupils' lives and experiences. Writing grows from oral language expression; thus, creative writing fits into the language experience sequence of communication, from thinking and speaking to writing and reading. Children cannot write imaginatively unless they have something to say. To teach creative writing, instruction must include experiences and exposure to the writing of others.

As children's reading programs become combined beyond the initial stages, creative writing provides the means of using pupils' thoughts and spoken language to further language development. As children make the

39

transition from dictated to independently written stories, pupils' stories are used less for developing reading vocabulary and more for fostering creative expression. Creative writing beyond the beginning stage does provide some reading material, making reading and writing personal and functional. The stories, however, are not the main body of reading materials at higher levels. Language study can develop from the original writing of pupils, and the writing experiences themselves can help pupils to put many language arts skills to use. The *use* of creative writing in the language experience approach involves more than the experience of writing itself.

Creative writing is not a separate or isolated activity but an integrated language experience in which children express thoughts, feelings, and experiences through written words. In creative writing, as in the experience stories, the process of communication is of greater importance than the finished product. In developing the children's power to write creatively, the teacher must present the children with the opportunities for self-expression and divergent thinking, and must provide the stimulation to release creativity as the children communicate their personal ideas through writing. The goals of creative writing experiences are to increase the power of written expression, to develop language awareness, and to provide stimuli and outlets for creativity. Vocabulary development should result from the opportunities to use words through writing. As children read the ideas of others, more experiences are available to them from which to create. The reader will note the interrelatedness of the chapters on vocabulary development, literature, and creative writing since these three types of language experiences are closely tied together, and attention to one area may involve the other areas as well.

In discussing creative writing in the language experience approach, it is necessary to examine how creative writing becomes a part of the total reading and language program. As children talk, as they encode, and as they read, the communication cycle in the language experience approach relies heavily on their writing. In Chapter 3 the focus was on experience stories which are a form of creative writing, but which tend to have more teacher direction in the early stages of instruction. At the higher levels, children having acquired more skills in handwriting and spelling can produce their own stories in creative forms. However, at these higher levels children may feel that they must conform to rigid standards or high expectations as to the correctness of form; therefore, they may not feel confident in their ability to be creative or may not feel that their efforts will be praised and accepted. At all levels the atmosphere which encourages, nurtures, and welcomes creative and original expression must be present if children are to grow in their ability to use written language expressively and effectively.

UNDERLYING PRINCIPLES
OF CREATIVE WRITING

Certain conditions foster creativity in children; others stifle it. Torrance has found that teacher personality and type of classroom environment affect the children's creative performance.[1] In developing an effective instructional program of creative writing, the following principles must be considered.

An atmosphere of acceptance and freedom is essential. Teachers must believe that each child has the potential to be creative. Climate and the process of self-expression are more important than a polished product. What children write must be accepted and valued by the teacher. Children must feel secure to venture new ideas, unusual thoughts, and experiment with written expression. All children in the elementary school cannot be expected to be gifted writers, and even children who write well will not always produce quality writing every time, but all children should feel that their contributions are accepted.

Evaluation of pupils' written expression should be on an individual basis. Creative writing must not be graded. Burrows writes, "The quality and sincerity of child writing dwindles to nothing if fear and self-consciousness set in."[2]. If children feel that set standards must be met each time they write and if their writing is to be graded, their freedom to create is blocked. Myers and Torrance talk of "time to think without being threatened by grades or tyrannized by time."[3] Evaluation occurs as children keep individual folders of stories and note improvements. Teachers may keep individual records of pupils' writing and note the qualities of originality, richness of expression, word quality, organization, and imagination. Occasionally classes will talk about qualities or characteristics

[1] E. Paul Torrance, *Guiding Creative Talent* (Englewood Cliffs, N. J.: Prentice-Hall, Inc., 1962).

[2] Alvina Burrows, Doris C. Jackson, and Dorothy O. Saunders, *They All Want to Write* (New York: Holt, Rinehart, & Winston, Inc., 1964), p. 43.

[3] R. E. Myers and E. Paul Torrance, *Teachers Guide, Invitations to Speaking and Writing Creatively* (Boston: Ginn and Company, 1965), p. v.

of good writing so that children will have some criteria for individual evaluation.

Children should be free to select their topics and to determine length and form. Since creative writing is personal, as the child puts down in *his* language what he feels and thinks, he selects the words used and the ideas communicated. When children write, topics should be open-ended with freedom of choice. Children should also have the option of choosing *not* to write.

Instruction in creative writing consists of more than having children record their thoughts in writing. Time must be spent on motivation, discussion, and sharing as well as on writing. Since children must have ideas and experiences from which to create, the teacher has a responsibility for providing experiences and models which children can draw upon for their own creative efforts. To develop pride of authorship, pupils need to share their writing with others and to have some of their stories and poems included in a class or individual book, a class newspaper, or in a bulletin board display.

Creative writing as defined in this chapter refers to that writing done by a child which is a reflection of his thoughts and experiences expressed in his choice of form and style. In her informative book on children's writing, Burrows makes a distinction between practical and personal writing.[4] Practical writing serves a functional purpose of communicating to others through letters, reports, or memos, and is basically informative or entertaining. Personal writing, however, is done to please the writer, and not necessarily to enlighten others. Even though practical writing can be creative and can contain some elements of individuality, in this chapter the focus is on creative writing of the imaginative and personal nature. While experience stories in the initial stages of instruction can be either practical or personal, at higher levels more stress is put on freeing creative expression.

In practical writing, when materials are designed to be read by others, there is a need for stressing spelling, punctuation, penmanship, and neatness. In the first draft of creative efforts, however, children should not be concerned with set standards. In creative writing experiences it is important that the child express in his language what he feels to be important. It is hoped that through many experiences with written expression children will apply the knowledge of punctuation, capitalization, spelling, and other mechanics of writing.

---

[4] Burrows, Jackson, and Saunders, *They All Want to Write*, pp. 2-5.

CONDUCTING CREATIVE WRITING EXPERIENCES

In planning creative writing experiences, the teacher must consider motivation, oral discussion before the actual recording, writing, the sharing of individual efforts, and, in some cases, subsequent or follow-up activities.

Teachers will find numerous suggestions for motivating creative writing in the supplementary readings cited at the end of this chapter. It should be stressed that one of the teacher's primary obligations in promoting creativity is to provide a supportive environment and to generate ideas and enthusiasm. Some of the proven means for encouraging thought on a particular topic are presenting a children's literature story or poem, showing some provocative pictures, asking stimulating questions, and suggesting imaginative topics. However, regardless of the motivation or technique used, children often are asked to write before thinking is truly stimulated. Thus, creative writing becomes an assignment instead of a language and thinking experience.

Oral discussions should be held before children are directed to write their ideas. Questions of "How does this look?" "How does it make you feel?" "What can you see, hear, or touch?" What are some interesting words you would want to use to describe what you see, hear, and feel?" stimulate thought. Children can react in an oral situation and can see that their responses are accepted. In the discussion the teacher should make many accepting comments such as, "That's a fine idea; you can use it in your story," or "That's an interesting way to describe what you feel. Can you include that when you write your ideas?" or "That's a sentence with lots of action; your story will probably be an exciting one." With comments of this nature, the children will feel encouraged to express their ideas. Another result of the discussion stage should be the realization that many types of stories are acceptable. Even though the motivation and discussion may have concentrated on a single theme, students are encouraged to develop that theme from various angles.

As children write their stories, the teacher can be available for help with words as needed. When a child asks how to spell a word, it is advisable for the teacher to write the word for him to copy. Every teacher is probably familiar with the situation in which a word is spelled orally, and the child asks her to repeat the spelling. The cards for the requested words can be put in the child's word bank, and the individual banks can be used as references during creative writing. With all the stress frequently put on the mechanics of writing and on the correctness of written work, it is recommended that the motivation for writing not be lessened by reminding children to spell and write correctly immediately before composing their stories. It is suggested that the teacher tell the children they can write about any of the ideas discussed or about something else if they wish. This type of comment emphasizes the open-ended dimension of the topic. Pupil choice must be respected. Generally, if an idea is well presented and appealing to children, they will be content to write about it. However, children should be free to approach any topic in a variety of ways or to write about something else if they choose to do so.

The sharing of creative writing provides a setting for functional listening, speaking, and oral reading. Small groups can be formed for pupils to read their stories to each other, or the teacher can read the stories to the group. Often when the teacher reads very expressively, children are surprised at how much their stories communicate. During the sharing periods, the teacher can comment on the good qualities of the stories mentioned in the oral discussion. Again, the focus is on acceptance and on language awareness stemming from the pupils' existing use of language. Sharing through displays should also be included. Collections of children's stories should be available in the classroom library and reading center, and stories can be taped and available in the listening center.

Description of a Sample Creative Writing Experience

Background information. The experience described here occurred in a fifth grade class, and the examples of the children's writing are exactly as they recorded them. In this example *The Sun is a Golden Earring* by Natalia Belting[5] was the only material needed other than pencils and paper for writing. In addition to the general objectives of developing creativity through writing and of enjoying literature, the objectives of this lesson were for children to be able:

1. To identify expressive words and phrases in order to develop language awareness.
2. To write a story or poem using descriptive words.
3. To express their thoughts in written language.

Motivation. The teacher introduced the book by explaining that *The Sun Is a Golden Earring* is a collection of short myths and legends from around the world about heavenly bodies and weather. These legends were told by ancient peoples to explain phenomena which they could not understand.

---

[5] Natalia Belting, *The Sun is a Golden Earring* (New York: Holt, Rinehart & Winston, Inc., 1962).

The title was discussed as a comparison, and the pupils were asked to listen for other comparisons in the book. The teacher wrote these questions: "What words help you see how something looks?" "What words tell how something sounds?" She then read the book aloud without any discussion during the reading.

Discussion. The teacher asked what comparisons the students noticed and they mentioned: "The sky is a tent roof," "The stars are a woman's necklace," and "The rainbow is a fishing line of the king of the dragons." The questions listed under motivation were discussed.

After talking about the book, the children were asked if they could describe the things in the sky or the kinds of weather. Gradually, pupils began to volunteer ideas. With each suggestion, praise and acceptance were given. Many times the teacher would say "That's an interesting description," or "That's a good word to use to describe the way that looks." The discussion was a warming-up period to help children formulate their ideas and realize that their suggestions would be accepted.

Writing. Before the children started to write, the teacher reminded them that they had expressed many good ideas which they could use in their stories or descriptions. The topic was open-ended, for it was suggested that they could write a brief explanation of how something in the sky came to be, or something about weather, or something entirely different if they wished.

As the children wrote, the teacher assisted with words which she wrote on small slips of paper for the children's word banks. In no case did she say, "Remember capital letters and punctuation." As she walked around, she made comments such as, "That's a good idea," "You describe that well," "You're off to a good start. Could you tell a little more how that happened or how it looks?" "That's a different idea," and "Good."

Reading. Children should decide whether or not their work is to be shared with others. In this lesson, the teacher collected the papers and said, "As I was watching you write, I saw many good stories and I think you would enjoy hearing them. When I come to your paper, will you tell me if I can read your story?" She then proceeded to call each child's name, to read the stories, and to comment favorably on some feature of each child's work. If a child said not to read his, that wish was respected but again a favorable comment was made. Interesting uses of words were noted by the teacher and the children during this sharing session.

Follow-up Activities. After the lesson described here, the children copied and illustrated their stories, which were used for a bulletin board

display. Some interesting words and phrases were added to the class compilation. (See page 53.) The book was available for individual reading. In order to provide additional experience with this type of writing, the writing center featured the question, "Can you write a legend about heavenly bodies or about the weather?"

Examples from a Fifth Grade Class

How an Ordinary God Made Lightning

Once a long time ago a very ordinary God wanted to talk to his friends in the sky. So he decided to go and try to talk to the Rain God. Now this very little meak God had never spoken a word before and wondered what it would be like. He thought for a while before he opened his mouth. He thought it might be like a trumpet or like the birds singing in the trees. But when he opened his mouth he found something very different. He could speak just like any other God but he had something specail. He found he could flash his teeth as he pleased for they were as bright as the Sun God. When He went to show the other Gods they said he must be the lightning God. And to this day when ever the lightning God talks there is lightning.

Lightning

There was and old lady who lives in the heavens. And all year long she would sit and sew. Sometimes she would drop her needle and it would fall and tear the sky. But then the sky was magic and after it was torn it would heal very quickly and that made Lightning.

Rain

Up in the heavens live an old man. All year long he would sit and smoke his pipe. When he was finished smoking he wouud shake the ashes out of his pipe. The ashes would fall to the earth. And this made Rain.

Snow and How It Became

Once there was a woman in the heavens who's husband was a god. One day her husband got up early and forgot to make his bed, so his wife had to make it. So she had to change the sheets and pillowcases. (because he slept on 15 pillows.) She went to shake the 15th pillow, which was the largest, and the seam came apart and the little tiny feathers flew down from the heavens. Now the god's wife had to go down and pick it up. And that is how the snow comes and goes.

The Story of Rain

One day a young and beautiful god was walking a long and saw a little boy pick and trample a beautiful flower. When she saw this she began to weep. Now every time a flower is picked anywhere she begins to weep. Her weeping is the rain.

Thunder and Lightning

Thunder is when the footplayers of both teams have the same score. And when one of the kickers of the team kicked the ball it sounded like thunder and it streeked through the sky like lightning and makes the winning point.

Snow

Snow is like a clean white sheet that has fallen across the United States and all the kids are happy. They take their sleds and other things.

Then the one of the old and meanest of all the sun gods took the sheet and wouldn't give it back till next winter.

Thunder, Rain, and, Lightning

One day some angles and some of the gods went bowling. The first angle missed and he started to cry. The next person was a god and he rooled the ball and sparks came and the Bang! all pins fell down the god was so happy the sun came out and the skies were clear again and all the people on earth were happy it stoped thundering, raining and lighting.

How Saturn Got its Rings

Once there was a great Queen who was very mean and she was very gready! She had a very huge chest of rings. In fact she had 100 for every finger. Thoe she was gready she was also as beautiful as the sunrise in the morning coming up over the montains. And she fell in love with a Prince, but he was not gready so he made her give up all her ring but 10 she didn't no what to do with them so she gave them to a planit called Saturn.

Rain

There was a god's wife who was peeling onions and the "fumes" made her cry. We call this rain.

Earth

There was a big turtle that walked in the heavens and one day died and fell into the space which took up the room of the earth and great vines grow and trees grow. Animales and a god lived there. We call it earth.

Hail

Someone from the heavens throwing rocks down to the earth.

The Moon and the Milky Way

Someone poured milk into the moon and it came out the bottom and fell into which we now call the Milky Way. The color white that you still see is the Milk stain which will stay there forever and ever.

How The Clouds Came to Be

The stars are a diamond teakettle and when the gods decide to have tea they boil the tea and steam comes out and forms the clouds.

How Rain, Thunder and Lighting is Caused

There was once a king who was mean and selfish. His palace was on the highest peak in the world. Whe he is mad he walks around and stampes his feet which caues thunder. He is so selfish he drank the all the water in the kingdon spilling haft the water which caues rain. The king's taxes were hight. Lighting was caused by the gold coins droping from his hand when he is counting it.

Thunder is like a stampid of elephants thundering across the heavens the lightning is there tails flashing across the sky.

Thundering

Thundering is two clouds smashing together. An horses feet claping in heaven And two people fighing and sceaming in heaven.

The Sound of a Horse

When a horse goes trotting in the lomesome dark streets, the hoofs sound like a man running from tearer. And when lighting strikes, the horse get's faster and faster intil it sounds like a a tribe of Indians having a war party.

How Rain Developed (a story of the gods)

One day when the earth was being formed it was very hot on earth. One day up in the heaven's a God was watering his lawn with a sprinkler The drops that hit the floor went through and some hissed. So they fell on the earth. Some were stuck in the web that separates earth from the heaven. They made the morning dew. Every time the Cheif God wanted rain he would call the man and tell him to turn on the sprinkler to water his lawn. Thats how rain developed
P. S. But of course he gets mean and doesn't turn it on. So we have a drought.

Thunder and Lightning

thunder—when a baseball Maneger and the Umpire are argueing and when a baseball player catches a line drive
lightning—when a baseball player hits a homerun and the ball streaks into the stands

When it rain's

1) When it rain's it's like a water sprinkler coming from the sky.
2) It's like dimes falling out of your pocket's, Like pennies gold and silver.

Thunder

I think thunder is when two mad scientists get angry when there out in the rain and shoot fifty calibre machine guns hit the clouds and the clouds yell.

Fog is from meteors coming close to earth. The used fuel from the fire on them comes into our atmosphere.

How snow looks to me

It is a God poping pop corn. He has a burning fire and pop corn is falling out. Poeple on earth are grabbing it and eating all they want.

Stars

Stars are white cookies that float in the sky. And Stars are big snow flakes.

Clouds

Clouds are smoke that travle under the sky, which is light.

Clouds And How They Were Formed

Clouds are like smoke from a chimney of a house in the heavens or a horse kiking up dust in the heavens.

What horses look like

Horses look like whitecaps on the dark blue sea. When the whitecaps swirl around madly, horses are galloping. When they're calm horses are trotting. Horses are so swift you can barely see their flying manes and tails which look like breezes blowing the green grass.

The Grass

The grass is like a slimy thin green snakes that have grown from the ground.

The procedure described in the preceding example was used with the book *The Long-Tailed Bear and Other Indian Legends* also by Natalia Belting.[6] The stories in this book are North American Indian tales or

---

[6] Natalia Belting, *The Long-Tailed Bear and Other Indian Legends* (Indianapolis: The Bobbs-Merrill Co., Inc., 1961).

"why" stories about animals. The following examples were written after fifth grade children heard "How the Cardinal Got His Red Feathers" taken from this collection.

How the Cat Got His Fur

One day there was only one cat in the world. It belong to a Barber. The cat always stood right under his masters feet. One day the Barber got a customer who had a lot of hair to be cut. First the Barber had to put a very sticky liquid on the man's head. By accident it fell on the cat so the Barber got another jar. He forgot to wipe the mess up and started cutting the man's hair. The cat rolled into the hair and it stuck tightly. That is how the cat got his fur.

How The Horse Got It's Tail And Mane or How The Horse Got Short Hair

The horse used to have a very long coat. He was shaggier than a English Sheep Dog. It was summer and as hot as a forest fire. The horse was very hot, so he went to the lion and asked him to cut his coat with his teeth. The lion agreed. It was very cool without his long coat. None of his hair grew back except where his mane and tail are.———The lion was magic and he knew that the horse would be cold in winter, so the horse's hair grows back in winter and he sheds in the summer

A White Rabbit and How it got its fur

A white rabbit it is so white it it looks like some snow has fallen on him. And he ran back to the forest and try to shake it off. but it couldn't come off. And it turn in to fur.

How the Fox got the white tip on his tail

A red fox which was as bright as the sunset was walking through the woods He decided to see "Man's House." So he he went their. "Man" had just finished painted his house snow white. He left the paint on the steps. Fox accidentally dipped the tip of his tail in the paint That's how the fox got his white tip.

P. S. ALL HER babies were born naturlly with white tips.

How the fox got his white tail

The fox was walking though the woods one day. He was very unhappy with his red tail because his red tail was like the red carnidel and the cat would come and jump on them. So he was walking though the wood one day when he saw a can labled white paint. So he dipped his tail in the paint and he thought that his whole body was white like the saimise cat. He was disapointed when he found out his body wasn't white. He told about it and they thought it looked nice so they dipped theirs in the white paint.

Why Spiders Have Six Legs and Why Some are black

Once there was a spider that had three children so, she had thre legs. She got the other three legs to mined her white washed web and to wash the dishes and answer the telephone. The nexed day her neighbor sent her child over to play. He was going to put black ink all over them He put black ink on the mother and one child but, he ran out of ink so, the others were brown because that was what coler they relly were.

The   End

How Our Hair Got its Color

Once apon a time there was a little girl with golden braids, named Audrey.

She was very curious and one day she asked her father why her hair was yellow.

Her father said, "Well, once there was a little girl with tan hair. She didn't like it she said it looked as though someone didn't wash it good enough.

One day her mother said, "Go outside and polish the silver lamp.

While she was polishing it a funny thing happened, smoke rose from it like someone was smoking a pipe inside it. A "jini" appeared and said "You have one wish.

She quickly said "I wish the fur on heads could be as yellow as the buttercups, as brown as the mud that lies on the earth, as black as the blackbirds or as red as the cardinal's wings are.

And to this very day those are still the colors of hair!

Other Teaching Suggestions

In a continuing program of creative writing, suggestions such as the following are appropriate.

Children can start a collection of the interesting language used in their stories. Using their words *verbatim* is an excellent practice since the children will then realize that they can say things in an expressive manner and that their expressions are valued by the teacher and by their classmates.

For example, in a second grade class, the children discussed what they would do if they had a hundred dollars to spend. In the individual stories written following the discussion, one boy wrote, "If I had a hundred dollars to spend I'd buy a bike so I could ride up and down the hills like the waves coming in fast." This simile was personal for this child who had had experiences at the nearby Chesapeake Bay. The group discussed why the comparison of the bike ride to the waves made the story more interesting than merely stating, "I'd ride up and down the hills." The sentence was placed on a chart labeled "Interesting Language," and other examples were added each time the group wrote stories. Another example was a description of giving a dog a bath, "His chin had a beard of soap suds." The children in this particular group were highly motivated to express their ideas in interesting ways and enjoyed having their expressions recognized by the total group.

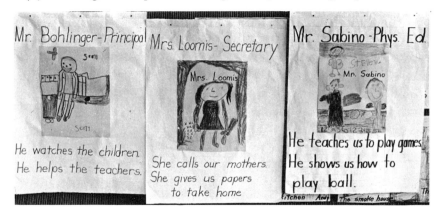

Read some literature to the children every day since creative writing can follow from certain selections. Children need exposure to the ideas of many authors. Discussion of the style, literary devices, and forms of writing can be developed from literature examples. (See Chapter 6.)

Alert pupils to the creative writing of children available in commercial publications. The books *Miracles*[7] and *The Wind and the Rain*[8] edited by Richard Lewis are excellent examples of children's writing in published form.

Collect the children's writing, and duplicate copies of a class book for each child. Children's stories and poems can be featured in class and school newspapers.

---

[7] Richard Lewis, compiler, *Miracles* (New York: Simon & Schuster, Inc., 1966).

[8] Richard Lewis, compiler, *The Wind and the Rain* (New York: Simon & Schuster, Inc., 1968).

Invite another class to hear the children read their original stories and poems.

Arrange attractive displays of the children's stories on bulletin boards and in the classroom reading center. Use children's stories for display purposes in the halls and in the school library.

A local author can visit the class to talk about the stages in developing a manuscript. Children can be alerted to the need for proofreading a final copy and can realize that polished copies come only after considerable rewriting.

For imaginative open-ended ways of stimulating productive thinking and imaginative writing, teachers will want to explore the teacher's guides and pupil idea books by Myers and Torrance. This series of *For Those Who Wonder, Invitations to Speaking and Writing Creatively,* and *Plots, Puzzles and Ploys* is published by Ginn and Company. Open-endedness, pupil involvement, and personal reaction and interpretation are distinctive features of all these materials. The directions and suggestions are helpful but not prescriptive.

Some Words of Caution

Teachers are sometimes alarmed about the lack of quality in children's writing, about the similarity of content in a particular child's stories, or about the tendency of children to imitate other children or a particular book or poem. While a teacher is concerned about these behaviors, the need is to convey an atmosphere of acceptance, to provide stimulation to create in a variety of situations, and to continue to offer exposure to a variety of models. While children's stories may not appear unique to adults, the teacher must look for that which is original and new for the child who is writing.

Children should have the opportunity to start over if they decide they do not like a particular story. They should also have the option of rough drafts, and it should be explained to them that frequently we have to rewrite a story to make the language and the ideas satisfactory. Children should not be forced to write on a particular day if none of the suggestions appeals to them. Attitude and interest are crucial, and demanding a composition may have many negative results.

Teachers will realize too that while many language experiences will not lead directly to creative writing, discussions of words, exposure to the language of literature, and encouraging reflective and divergent thinking are the foundation for imaginative writing.

The feeling we want children to have toward creative writing is expressively stated by a student in one of the author's classes who watched a creative writing demonstration with children and then composed the following poem.

Show Me The Way

Oh, the comfort—
The inexpressible comfort of feeling
accepted by my teacher,
Having woven my thoughts into an idea,
Not to judge or measure—but
pouring them all out—
Just as they are—polished and rough together—
Certain that an understanding hand
will take and sift them all,
Keep what is worth keeping,
And with a breath of praise
Show me the way.

SUMMARY

Creative writing experiences contribute to the language experience approach to teaching communication skills. Through the recording of original thoughts in written language, children are creating personal reading materials which can lead to further language study. The teacher's responsibility is to provide an accepting atmosphere and the stimulation of the encouragement of pupil writing. A directed creative writing experience includes motivation, oral discussion, recording by children, and in some cases, sharing of individual creative efforts with other children.

Creative writing seeks to encourage the process of expressing thoughts in original and fresh ways thereby increasing the power of using language. The experience is more important than the product. If creative writing is to be successful, the atmosphere must encourage creativity in all areas. The personality and attitudes of the teacher determine the children's freedom to create.

SUGGESTED READINGS

Applegate, Mauree, *Easy in English*. Evanston, Ill.: Row, Peterson and Company, 1962. Applegate discusses creativity in relation to all of the language arts. As teachers read her book, they will note many suggestions for developing children's power to write creatively.

Burrows, Alvina, Doris C. Jackson, and Dorothy O. Saunders, *They All Want to Write.* New York: Holt, Rinehart & Winston, 1964. Every teacher who works with creative writing should be familiar with this book which clearly elaborates the philosophy regarding writing experiences. The many examples of children's writing add to the impact of the content.

Petty, Walter T. and Mary Bowen, *Slithery Snakes and Other Aids to Children's Writing.* New York: Appleton-Century-Crofts, 1967. This paperback book contains both theoretical and practical information for the teacher who is interested in providing a dynamic creative writing program. Numerous topics for writing are suggested, and examples of children's work are included.

Walter, Nina Willis, *Let Them Write Poetry.* New York: Holt, Rinehart & Winston, 1964. Walter's paperback book explores poetry writing from the kindergarten through high school. Examples of children's writing are included, and the examples for developing awareness of poetic expression, of imagery, and of word quality are particularly well-described.

Yamamoto, Kaoru, *Experimental Scoring Manuals for Minnesota Tests of Creative Thinking and Writing.* Kent, Ohio: Bureau of Educational Research, Kent State University, May, 1964, pp. 102-158. A scoring guide for evaluating the "creativity" of imaginative stories written by children in grades 3-6. Six categories of criteria (organization, sensitivity, originality, imagination, psychological insight, richness of expression) are discussed and illustrative examples are included.

CHAPTER FIVE

Vocabulary Development in the Language Experience Approach

"What are words?
Words are how what you think inside comes out
And how to remember what you might forget about."
from *Sparkle and Spin*[1]

To say we speak, listen, read, and write with words seems to be stating an all too obvious fact. Even though, is it not also essential to provide planned, directed experiences for developing children's facility with words? To give experience form and substance, children need tools or words for translating events into language. A command of vocabulary is a necessity for conveying and receiving thoughts, feelings, and emotions. If children are to be equipped to put their thoughts into speech or writing and equipped to understand the thoughts of speakers and authors, they must be equipped with the word knowledge these language tasks require.

Extending children's word meanings presents a major focus of instruction in developing the facility to communicate in both spoken and written language. The goals of such instruction are to increase the stock of words used by individuals in their listening, speaking, reading, and writing, to promote awareness of fine

---

[1] Paul Rand and Ann Rand, *Sparkle and Spin* (New York: Harcourt, Brace & World, Inc., 1957).

shades of meaning, and to develop an attitude of interest in words. Applegate shows the results of these goals in an anecdote about a fourth grader who told his teacher: "Why, we don't have to be just *mad* anymore. We've learned new words, and now we can be *angry, frustrated, irritated, or furious."*[2]

Word knowledge has been found to be one of the most significant factors in reading comprehension, while a limited vocabulary presents an obstacle to effective comprehension in reading.[3] The more fluent a child is in oral vocabulary, the greater his resources for associating meaning with printed words. Davis reports that one of the major obligations in teaching comprehension is to make pupils familiar with the meanings of as many words as possible.[4] However, word study should be done in meaningful context within sentence patterns. The language experience approach provides this meaningful context.

In building children's vocabularies, attention must be directed to increasing each of the four types of vocabulary (listening, speaking, reading, and writing). Increased understanding of words in one facet of the language arts should add to understanding in the other facets. In fact, the language experience approach with its integration of the expressive and receptive facets of language provides experiences which contribute to vocabulary development in all areas.

A basic distinction of vocabulary study in the language experience approach is that *the language study stems from the children's oral and written language expression.* In other words, instead of starting with a list of words or passages from language arts textbooks as examples for study, the words selected originate in the children's speech, in their stories, and in their word banks. Word power will grow as children encounter situations in which they need to communicate. In word study, as in all aspects of language experience learning, practical application is the base from which language develops. John Holt states that, "What we have to recognize is . . . that it is the effort to use words well, to say what he wants to say, to people whom he trusts, and wants to reach and move, that alone will teach a young person to use words better."[5]

Research supports the importance of personal meaning and motivation in vocabulary learning. Olson and Pau found that children re-

---

[2] Mauree Applegate, *Easy in English* (Evanston, Illinois: Row, Peterson and Company, 1962), p. 29.

[3] Frederick Davis, "Research in Comprehension in Reading," *Reading Research Quarterly*, III, (Summer, 1968), 508.

[4] *Ibid.*, p. 543.

[5] John Holt, "Introduction" in Herbert Kohl, *Teaching the "Unteachable"* (New York: The New York Review, 1966), p. 9.

quired significantly fewer trials to learn highly emotional words than were required to learn words without strong emotional associations.[6]

Sylvia Ashton-Warner who achieved phenomenal success in working with Mauri children of New Zealand called her work with reading vocabulary "key vocabulary" as she made use of personal word files. She communicates the necessity for personal involvement in the learning as she describes the child who stalled for months on the words, *come, look, and,* and then learned *police, butcher knife, kill, gaol, hand,* and *fire engine* in four minutes in response to the question of what he feared.[7] The *words he wanted to learn* were used to teach him to read.

WHAT CONCEPTS DO CHILDREN NEED TO DEVELOP ABOUT WORDS?

Not only should children use words effectively with ever-increasing vocabularies, but they should have an understanding of how words convey meaning in our language. The following list identifies some basic concepts which should be developed with elementary children.

1. Words help express our thoughts. In order to develop vocabulary as well as any language skill, pupils must see the need for communication in functional settings. Word study should help children understand the interrelationships of speaking, listening, reading, and writing. Pupils should discover that the words they speak can be written and read. They should discover, too, that the words of others can be written and spoken.

2. The exact meaning of a word is dependent upon the use of the words in context. Vocabulary study must be in connection with the language patterns in which the words occur. Lefevre, a noted linguist, believes that the sentence, not the word, is the smallest unit of meaning in our language.[8] Word study must deal with words used in contextual settings. As children discuss multiple meanings, it is easy to illustrate that the exact meaning of a word cannot be determined apart from the context in which it is used. Developing an awareness of fine shades of meaning and selecting

---

[6] David R. Olson and A. S. Pau, "Emotionally Loaded Words and the Aquisition of a Sight Vocabulary," *Journal of Educational Psychology*, LVII, (June, 1966), 174-178.

[7] Sylvia Ashton-Warner, *Teacher* (New York: Simon & Schuster, Inc., 1966), p. 43.

[8] Carl A. Lefevre, *Linguistics and the Teaching of Reading* (New York: McGraw-Hill Book Company, 1964), p. 6.

the most appropriate word for the meaning intended must be fostered.

3. Some meanings can be expressed by more than one word. Children should be alerted to synonyms as one means of increasing word power. As children work with their individual word boxes and as a group compiles class word banks, there will be many examples of synonyms.

4. In English there are specific functions of words in the syntactical patterns of the language. Lefevre identifies two word classifications, full words and empty words. The full words are those which have specific meanings or referents, while empty words are those without a concrete referent. Words such as *the, which,* and *and* are examples of the approximately 300 empty words of English.[9] Children can understand the four word classes noun, verb, adjective, and adverb only as these classes occur in sentence patterns. Activities with sentence building and the discussion of sentences used in children's writing can illustrate language structure and word functions in sentence patterns. Effective use of vocabulary for the reception and expression of ideas, not the terminology, is the purpose of vocabulary instruction.

TYPES OF VOCABULARY

In discussing children's vocabularies, it is again necessary to look at the four dimensions of the language arts. Children have more than one type of vocabulary, and teachers must be concerned with the development of each type. A child's listening vocabulary is composed of those words which he can understand when others use them although he may not use them in his own speech or recognize them in print. A child has a speaking vocabulary which is composed of those words which he can use in his oral language. As a child learns to read, he acquires a reading vocabulary which is composed of those words which he can recognize in printed form and with which he can associate a meaning. As a child learns to write and spell, he acquires a writing vocabulary. In the early elementary years the listening vocabulary is the largest, the speaking vocabulary is next, then reading, then the writing vocabulary last. The reading vocabulary will surpass the speaking vocabulary in the fourth and fifth grades for those children progressing well in reading.[10]

9 *Ibid.*, pp. 9-10.
10 David H. Russell, *Children Learn to Read* (Boston: Ginn and Company, 1961), p. 266.

In the language experience approach, the listening, speaking, reading, and writing vocabularies are extended through activities with group and individual word banks, through literature experiences, and through writing and speaking activities. In the elementary school concern with reading and writing has overshadowed the teaching of listening and speaking. In vocabulary instruction, stress must be placed on listening and speaking as well as on written language.

Individual Word Banks

Word banks or files kept by individual pupils are one of the major types of material in the language experience approach. An individual word bank is a personal vocabulary file kept by each pupil and used in a variety of ways for promoting vocabulary development and language awareness. A word is put into the word bank after it has been used in an oral or written sentence pattern. In the initial stages of reading instruction, the word banks are used primarily to reinforce the learning of sight vocabulary. As children progress in reading skills, individual word banks can be used as a reference for spelling and writing activities and for oral language discussions about words. In this section, the word banks will be discussed first in relation to beginning reading instruction and then in relation to other types of language study.

The major functions of the individual word banks are:

1. To serve as a record of the reading vocabulary of individual students.
2. To serve as references for creative writing and spelling.
3. To provide reinforcement through repeated exposure to words.
4. To serve as stimulus words for examples for skill instruction.
5. To provide independent activities with word games, matching activities, sentence building.
6. To provide examples for group language study.

Questions frequently asked by teachers about word banks are: "How is a word bank started?" "What format is the most practical?" "How can words be classified?" "How can the word banks be used for independent activities?" "How can the word banks be used for directed language study?"

Starting Individual Word Banks The simplest way of starting individual word banks with a class is in connection with either a group experience story or a personal experience story. Any word which a child can identify can be written for his word bank. For example, if the class has composed a group experience story about the classroom pet, a hamster, one child may be able to read the words *hamster* and *brown*. If so, these words will be placed on cards for his word bank. Another child may be able to read the words *hamster, little,* and *eat.* These three words are written for this child's word file. Each child will choose different words, and the teacher should not attempt to have a group of pupils select identical words for mastery.

The same procedure can be followed when working with individual experience stories. The child may be asked to underline the words in his story which he knows. Again, these words are written on cards for his word bank. These word cards will be used for many of the activities described later in this chapter.

Other procedures may be used for starting or adding to the individual word banks. In the beginning stages of reading, pupils' names can be used to arouse curiosity about words. The first word in a child's bank could be his name. As pupils learn to read the names of their classmates, these words could be included in the word banks. Pupils may learn some words from signs and from bulletin board captions around the room. The teacher will explain to the group that if they can read those words, cards will be placed in their banks.

Another source for starting or for adding to the word banks is children's literature. After reading a story to the class the teacher may ask, "What was the most interesting word you heard in this story?" or "What word in the story would you like to know?"

Some cautions should be noted regarding the above procedures. The teacher should not be in a hurry to have children add too many words to the banks since this may lead to confusion. The rate of learning will differ from pupil to pupil, and the purpose of word banks should not be viewed by pupils as collecting as many words as possible.

Opportunities for re-reading and for repeated exposure to words should be provided, especially in the initial stages of instruction. Teachers should not be upset when children occasionally forget a word. In working with commercial reading materials, children will also forget words. Re-teaching is in order in both cases. In the language experience approach, re-teaching or extra practice can be provided by having the child find the sentence in the story in which he first used the word and by having him write the sentence and underline the word. The child can talk about the meaning of the word and match the card from the bank to the word in the story. One category of words in a bank can be "Words I Need to Work On," and a missed word can be placed in this category. The child can be directed to build a sentence using the forgotten word with cards from the word bank.

Another caution regarding the word banks relates to the selection of words. Children, not the teacher, should select the words they wish to know. However, the teacher may ask, "Do you know this word? It is a word you will use in many stories." Some teacher suggestions may be offered, but the selection of the words in the individual word banks remains the child's choice.

Group Word Banks

Word banks can be developed with an entire class or with sub-groups within a class. Generally in most classes, there will be many group word banks for various categories of word study. In the group word banks greater attention is placed on general language development and less on reading vocabulary in contrast with individual word banks.

The functions of the group word banks are:

1. To develop language awareness and interest in word study.
2. To focus language study on word categories and functions.
3. To serve as a reference (a type of class dictionary) for word study or as a spelling check when doing independent writing.
4. To provide materials for independent activities with words.

Starting Group Word Banks In developing group word banks, discussions and group experience stories will be the main sources of words. The easiest way of initiating group banks with any class is to discuss word categories such as colors, animals, naming words, and so on. For example, in kindergarten or first grade, the first group word file could be an outgrowth of a group experience story. If the pupils have written a story about the colors of the fall leaves, they could be asked to find all the words which name colors. These words could then be written on cards and placed in a box or envelope labeled "color words." If the children have written some chart stories about animals, they could reread these stories and find all the words which name animals and include this classification in a word file. Numerous categories can and should be used.

The meanings of words in the group files should be familiar to pupils, and the words added to the word banks should have been used in the talk and writing of the class so that the first encounter with a word was in a contextual setting. The cards for the group banks can include a sentence definition or a picture with each word. Teachers may wish to number the group experience stories and have a folder of typed copies available in the classroom writing center. This folder should include an envelope of word bank cards which are numbered according to the story in which the words were used.

Format of the Word Banks No single format is satisfactory to all teachers. Regardless of the arrangement, the bank should permit easy reclassification of words, should be organized so children can locate a particular word quickly, and should be styled for easy manipulation during independent study. Boxes with each word on a separate card or slip of paper are recommended. A notebook type of listing does not have the feature of easy manipulation or reclassification. Teachers generally find that oak tag or other relatively heavy paper increases the durability of the word cards. Many teachers find that index cards are easy to use and to file in either a standard size file box or in cardboard boxes from a department store. Some teachers report that the cardboard boxes are quieter than the metal ones!

A card of 1″ x 2″ is generally adequate for individual use, especially if pupils are going to build sentences at their desks. Also, a small card is more satisfactory for comparison with a word in an individual experience story. During the beginning stages, a teacher may prefer using large word cards and shoe boxes for files.

Providing envelopes for classification into such categories as "color words," "naming words," or "letters of the alphabet" is helpful. Many ways of classifying words should be used and changed throughout the school year.

The group word banks may utilize 4″ x 6″ or 6″ x 8″ index cards for visibility by the total group. These can be contained in shoe boxes or larger file boxes in the writing center. Again, envelopes for classification are useful, and as the files expand beyond the first grade level, a separate box can be used for each category. For example, there may be a group word bank of synonyms, another of antonyms, another for words with multiple meanings, another for descriptive words, and another for interesting language expressions, word pictures, and similes or metaphors.

Activities with Word Banks

One of the major advantages of the word banks for language study is their adaptability to many types of activities. The classification activity, which is one of the most valuable, can begin very early in the reading and language arts instruction by varying the level and categories according to the children's maturity. Perhaps the simplest means of classification is by alphabetical order. While this is a useful and practical means of locating words easily, the classification of words should not be limited to filing entries in alphabetical order. Language study will be much more appropriate if children study word qualities, definitions, and functions.

As an example of introducing the classification of words at the beginning reading level, a teacher could ask a small group of children to bring their word banks to the reading table and find words which name things. These words could then be examined for those which name people, food, or animals. Another time children could be directed to find all the words which are action or descriptive words. The labeling of nouns, verbs, and other parts of speech is unimportant. What is important is that the children understand how words function in a sentence context to convey meaning.

Word banks can lead to the discussions of word categories and then to the development and extension of each category. The teacher can ask the pupils to find the most interesting words in their banks and tell why a particular word is interesting to them. In one first grade class, a girl volunteered *glitter* and *sparkle* as her most interesting words. These words had been used in a story describing her Halloween costume. Another child said that *diesel engine* and *blast-off* were his most interesting words. The practice of identifying interesting words can contribute considerably to language awareness.

Children will be introduced to many types of classification as they progress in reading, and teachers will find word banks extremely useful for working with multiple meanings, synonyms, antonyms, homonyms, and other categories. Any classification should change as the children realize that a particular word may fit in a number of categories depending upon its use in context.

Word banks can be used for sentence building activities as a child or a group of children combines the words in different patterns. The word banks can provide the basis for work with kernel sentences and their extension with additional words. For example, two words such as "Boy jumped" or "Cat ate" can be selected from a bank and the children can be asked to find words which might describe the boy or the cat, words which tell how the boy jumped or what the cat ate. Children can select two words for kernel sentences and ask their classmates to add to the original sentence. When this activity uses the word banks, children are working with *their* language as they extend their knowledge of how words function in sentence patterns.

Word banks are practical for independent reading and language activities. Children can work in pairs or teams as they read each other's words and stories or as they build sentences with the word cards. Some children may want to compile individual dictionaries by writing definitions for the words in their banks.

Children should be encouraged to refer to both the individual and group word banks when doing creative writing. Writing can be motivated by having children select words from the bank to make an interesting title, and then they can write a story for that title. In connection with

the study of word categories, children could write a story using as many words of a particular category as possible.

In the classroom writing center, described in Chapter 9, word banks should be available for reference for independent writing and independent language study.

Possibilities for group word banks include the following:

Descriptive words	Compound words
Naming words	Words for said
Action words	Words with prefixes
Interesting words	Words with suffixes
Words for sounds	Synonyms
Words for colors	Homonyms
Words for animals	Science words
Opposites	Three syllable words
Words with more than one meaning	Four syllable words
Social studies words	

OTHER ACTIVITIES FOR WORD STUDY

Pupils in the intermediate grades can extend and deepen their study of words by probing into the origins of words. Perhaps the class can keep banks of words with interesting origins. Dictionary study can be helpful with this activity as students are alerted to the information about word origins to be found in a dictionary. The brief pamphlet, *Pageant of Words*,[11] published by Scott, Foresman and Company, has a number of suggestions for studying word origins and includes the names of appropriate trade books related to word study.

A notebook could be kept on the writing center table or in the reading center for pupil use in recording interesting words found in their independent reading. They can also keep personal lists of these words.

Activities with literature and creative writing also promote vocabulary growth, and the reader is directed to Chapters 4 and 6 for other ideas relating to vocabulary.

SUMMARY

Increasing children's listening, speaking, reading, and writing vocabularies receives major attention in the language experience approach. Opportunities to use words in personal communication situations in speaking and writing provide the best means for developing word power. In the language experience approach, many opportunities for discussion of words will occur, and developing an awareness of words should be a continuing goal. In vocabulary development as in other concerns in the language experience approach, the three characteristics of pupil-composed materials, the interrelationships of all the language arts, and the lack of vocabulary control are apparent.

Through language experience activities children should discover many ways of using words for communication. Individual and group word banks constitute a major tool for vocabulary study as they are used as a record of words learned and as materials for numerous other language activities. The teachers' responsibility is to provide the setting and the stimuli for word study growing from the child's own language.

---

11 *Pageant of Words* (Glenview, Illinois: Scott, Foresman and Company, 1966).

SUGGESTED READINGS

Applegate, Mauree, *Easy in English*. Evanston, Ill.: Row, Peterson and Company, 1962, Chapter 2. Applegate conveys the message of the chapter title, "Words Make the Difference" perceptively and includes activities for extending vocabulary in creative ways.

Ashton-Warner, Sylvia, *Teacher*. New York: Simon & Schuster, Inc., 1963. The description of the "key vocabulary" in teaching reading shows the use of individual word files for vocabulary. The reader will note the emotional impact of the words selected by Mrs. Ashton-Warner's pupils.

Glaus, Marlene, *From Thoughts to Words*. Champaign, Ill.: National Council of Teachers of English, 1965. This paperback book is a collection of ideas for the classroom teacher who wants to combine creativity and language expression.

Tiedt, Iris M. and Sidney W. Tiedt, *Contemporary English in the Elementary School*. Boston: Allyn & Bacon, Inc., 1967, Chapter 3. The chapter on word study contains many activities which can be utilized for developing an interest in word study.

CHAPTER SIX

Literature as a Language Experience

Literature as a language experience presents opportunities for developing children's language facility in personal, communicative, creative, and functional ways. The place of literature in an elementary reading program is generally accepted as being of utmost significance in promoting pleasurable experiences with reading, thereby contributing to the development of a permanent interest in and favorable attitudes toward reading. The values of literature for entertainment, for extending experience backgrounds, and for developing self-understanding and understanding of others have been well-elaborated by a number of authorities on children's literature.[1, 2, 3] However, the contribution of literature as a language enriching experience needs greater attention than it currently receives in many classrooms. The freshness and originality of language in children's literature is one of its unique qualities that no other materials or curriculum experiences can offer.

Literature is a *personal* language experience since children respond to stories in individual ways and express

[1] May Hill Arbuthnot, *Children and Books* (Chicago: Scott, Foresman and Company, 1964).

[2] Charlotte S. Huck and Doris Y. Kuhn, *Children's Literature in the Elementary School* (New York: Holt, Rinehart & Winston, Inc., 1968).

[3] Leland B. Jacobs, "Children's Experiences With Literature," in *Children and the Language Arts* (Englewood Cliffs, N. J.: Prentice-Hall, Inc., 1955), 192-217.

their reactions to characters, plots, and themes in terms of their individual background. In encouraging divergent reactions to stories read to children and to those which they read for themselves, questions such as, "How did *you* feel?" "What would *you* have done?" "What did this story make *you* think of?" will permit and encourage a variety of responses.

Literature is a *communicative* language experience because children use the receptive language skills of listening and reading in order to absorb ideas. Through discussion of literature and writing about literature, the expressive facets of the language arts are employed.

Literature is a *creative* language experience when it serves as a stimulus for creative thinking and leads to the production of creative stories and poems by children.

Literature is a *functional* language experience since children clearly perceive a purpose to activities with literature and since with these activities listening, speaking, reading, and writing are related to content of high interest and meaning. The creative, personal, and communicative attributes contribute to the purposefulness of the literature experiences.

The theme of this chapter is the interrelatedness of language experiences and literature. At all levels in the elementary school, there is a place for experiences with literature which expand vocabulary, which build awareness of writing styles, and which stimulate creative writing. Questions to be examined include: How can literature be used to develop communication skills? How can literature be used to promote vocabulary growth? How can literature be used to develop awareness of styles of writing? How can children's literature be used in the language experience framework of going from speech to recording to reading as pupils create reading materials?

Throughout the chapter, books which are especially applicable in relating literature to other language experiences are cited. The reader will note too that in the chapter on vocabulary development and creative writing, references are also made to literature since these three topics are closely interwoven.

THE TEACHER'S ROLE

The teacher must provide the time, the motivation, and the materials for children to explore the possibilities of developing language awareness through literature. In a study of children's reading preferences and habits, Helen Huus found that the adults in the environment were a significant factor affecting interest in reading.[4] As the significant adult in the school environment, the teacher must provide the model of valuing literature. Experiences with literature are essential in any good reading program. In all classrooms the following experiences should be included:

1. The daily reading aloud of a children's literature selection by the teacher.

2. A classroom library corner or table where books are displayed attractively and changed frequently.

3. Opportunities for children to examine books as an independent activity.

4. Regularly scheduled time for independent reading.

5. A minimum of a weekly class visit to the school library during which each child can check out a book of his own choosing.

6. Opportunities for individuals to use the library as needed in addition to the regularly scheduled visit.

In addition to the previously listed types of experiences the teacher must offer activities with literature which contribute directly to the language experience reading program.

The major purpose in reading literature to children and in encouraging personal reading is to have them enjoy stories. Never should the enjoyment be overlooked as literature is used to contribute to the total language program in some of the ways discussed in this chapter. However, it cannot be assumed that children will become aware of writing styles or of the creative use of language without some direct guidance by the teacher.

The teacher's responsibilities include knowing many books, developing some techniques for alerting children to language through literature, and providing opportunities for children to use models from literature to express their own ideas in spoken and written language.

HOW CAN LITERATURE STIMULATE LANGUAGE AWARENESS?

Language quality is one of the hallmarks of good literature. One of the reasons literature belongs in the elementary curriculum is simply that it is imaginative language. Jacobs talks about "colorful, tongue-

---

4 Helen Huus, "Interpreting Research in Children's Literature," in *Children, Books and Reading, Perspectives in Reading No.* 3 (Newark, Delaware: International Reading Association, 1964), p. 127.

tickling words and neatly turned phrases" which are a part of story-telling.[5] Through literature, children can experience examples of the creative use of language in a very natural informal way. It is hoped that through exposure to the language of literature children will extend their ability to use language expressively. Exposure to models of original and creative expression by gifted authors is essential if real language awareness and power is to develop in the elementary years. In using literature with children, we want them both to hear and read the best that has been written and to express their own thoughts and ideas. During the early school years, when children's reading skills are minimal, hearing literature read aloud is their major exposure to the imaginative use of language. Children's literature materials can serve as a motivation for the creation of pupil-composed materials and can help to lead pupils from spoken language to written language.

Although children will have more experiences with prose literature than with poetry, poetry also can stimulate language awareness and creative responses in children. The imagery, the figurative language, and the brevity of thought can add to the appeal of this branch of literature. Interest, enjoyment, appreciation, and a love for poetry can be nurtured by reading many examples aloud. The teacher should be familiar with anthologies and should develop personal anthologies of his own favorites. He can seek to build an awareness of mood, of visual and auditory imagery, and emotional responses through exposure to poetry. In the following sections on creative writing, vocabulary development, and author's style, examples are drawn from both prose and poetry. The same methodology can be used with each.

HOW CAN LITERATURE LEAD
TO CREATIVE WRITING?

One of the major applications of literature in the total language curriculum is as an impetus for creative writing. Through the awareness of language, development of vocabulary, and understanding of style, the tools for personal writing are acquired.

If we expect children to write creatively, do we not need to provide exposure and awareness of the creative use of language and of the thoughts of other authors? The input of ideas and of expressive language

---

[5] Jacobs, "Children's Experiences With Literature," p. 198.

must be a part of any children's program which seeks to develop the power to communicate in both spoken and written language. The input of ideas through literature is vital if children are going to have a reservoir of knowledge for their own creativity.

As pupils hear and read models of prose and types of poetry, they can be stimulated to write their own stories and poems. For example, fables, tall tales, and haiku are excellent models. Examples of haiku poetry can be found in *Cricket Songs* by Harry Behn[6] and *In A Spring Garden* by Richard Lewis.[7] As in all creative writing, the thought is more important than the form. In haiku poetry the seventeen syllable form can be discussed, but attention should be given to the thoughts expressed instead of to the number of syllables included.

Children's literature can lead to many types of writing about books in addition to the creative formulation of stories and poems. The following are suggested as ways for children to share independent reading with each other through writing.

Written book reports of a routine type are not in harmony with the personal, communicative, creative, and functional philosophy of the language experience approach. However, certain types of writing about books should be encouraged. Children can be introduced to book reviews through newspapers and periodicals and should experiment with this style of writing. They can try writing personal reviews of their favorite books to interest others in a particular book. Book reviews can be featured in the class newspaper or collected and displayed in the classroom reading corner.

Children can write about and to their favorite authors, and they can share their writing about books in small interest groups and with members of other classes. Character sketches and descriptions for book jackets are other types of writing about books.

In each type of writing, the teacher should first introduce a model to the children. For example, in working with the writing of book jacket descriptions, the teacher could read the children the blurbs from several familiar jackets, and the class could compose together a description for another jacket. Then the children could write individual blurbs to interest other children in the book.

For young children, literature can lead to the creation of group experience charts, individual experience stories, and group books discussed

---

6 Harry Behn, compiler, *Cricket Songs* (New York: Harcourt, Brace & World, Inc., 1964).

7 Richard Lewis, compiler, *In a Spring Garden* (New York: The Dial Press, Inc., 1965).

in Chapter 3. A group book of pages describing children's reactions to favorite stories could be used with kindergarten and first grade children as they dictate their comments.

At the primary grade levels, reading a story aloud to children can be the stimulus for a group to dictate stories about a similar topic. For example, if children listen to the story *Swimmy* by Leo Lionni,[8] they can write stories about fish or after hearing the story *Rufus* by Tomi Ungerer,[9] they could dictate stories about bats.

Hearing a story read aloud can lead to the writing of a group experience story as the children dictate their reactions to a story or write a summary of the plot. The chart could be made to interest another class in a book.

HOW CAN LITERATURE DEVELOP AWARENESS OF WRITING STYLES?

Style is the quality which makes a piece of writing distinctive and individual. Arbuthnot describes style as ". . . difficult to define, a quality of which children are unconscious and yet one to which they respond as surely as they respond to a smile."[10] Exposure to various writing styles in literature develops the concept of adapting language to one's ideas which is basic to the goal of helping children to use language more effectively.

In analyzing style, children should be alerted to certain techniques used by writers. The introduction of these techniques can best be illustrated by their occurrence in literature. Studying authors' styles should be carried over to pupils' writing by providing numerous experiences for writing in different moods or for employing different techniques.

Petty and Bowen identify personification, onomatopoeia, alliteration, and internal rhyme as devices which can be easily learned and applied by elementary pupils.[11] Children need not learn the technical names for

---

[8] Leo Lionni, *Swimmy* (New York: Pantheon Books, Inc., 1963).
[9] Tomi Ungerer, *Rufus* (New York: Harper & Row, Publishers, 1961).
[10] Arbuthnot, *Children and Books*, p. 18.
[11] Walter T. Petty and Mary E. Bowen, *Slithery Snakes and Other Aids to Children's Writing* (New York: Appleton-Century-Crofts, 1967), pp. 64-70.

these techniques but should recognize them when they occur in literature and use them in their own writing.

Personification can be pointed out to young children as they recognize the human characteristics attributed to non-human objects in stories like *Mike Mulligan and His Steam Shovel*[12] and *The Little House*,[13] both by Virginia Burton, and *Little Toot*,[14] *Loopy*,[15] and *Hercules*[16] by Hardy Gramatky. Many other examples of personification exist in children's literature selections. Pupils can be asked to write stories using personification.

In a clinic situation with remedial readers, the grab bag technique was used to have children experiment with personification. A number of objects were placed in the grab bag and the children were asked to pick one and then write a story beginning with "I am . . ." Teachers can ask children to compose a story with an object as the main character.

As appropriate examples occur in the poetry read to children, the teacher may comment on the auditory qualities which make particular poems distinctive. Comments such as, "When you write a poem, you might want to use several words which begin alike in a line," or "You might want to try to find words which sound like the idea the word represents," are good examples.

In alerting children to the mood of stories, serious and light stories on the same topic can be read to children for contrast. Children can also identify the words used by an author to create a certain mood. For example, children could compare the mystical mood in *Where Does the Butterfly Go When It Rains?* by May Garelick[17] with the factual descriptions in *Rain Drop Splash* by Alvin Tresselt.[18] Children at upper grade levels can discuss the differences in mood between various books read in their independent study.

The concern is not to develop set techniques or styles for pupils but through exposure and discussion to have children realize that style changes according to the content, the purpose of the writing, the mood, and the author. Children should grasp the concept that different authors have different styles just as in class they have different styles. We can

---

12 Virginia Burton, *Mike Mulligan and His Steam Shovel* (Boston: Houghton Mifflin Company, 1939).

13 Virginia Burton, *The Little House* (Boston: Houghton Mifflin Company, 1942).

14 Hardy Gramatky, *Little Toot* (New York: G.P. Putnam's Sons, 1939).

15 Hardy Gramatky, *Loopy* (New York: G.P. Putnam's Sons, 1939).

16 Hardy Gramatky, *Hercules* (New York: G.P. Putnam's Sons, 1940).

17 May Garelick, *Where Does the Butterfly Go When It Rains?* (New York: William R. Scott, Inc., 1963).

18 Alvin Tresselt, *Rain Drop Splash* (New York: Lothrop, Lee & Shepard Co., Inc., 1946).

encourage children to experiment in their writing by accepting their language, by giving them opportunities to discuss styles of writing in literature examples, and by providing situations for them to employ different styles and techniques in their personal writing.

HOW CAN LITERATURE CONTRIBUTE TO THE DEVELOPMENT OF VOCABULARY?

The fact that continued exposure to the language of others results in the development of speaking vocabulary is well-documented by studies of the acquisition of oral language in the young child as he learns to speak from hearing the language of those in his environment. Exposure to the words of literature also adds to a child's vocabulary development. However, in addition to the informal exposure offered by literature, some steps

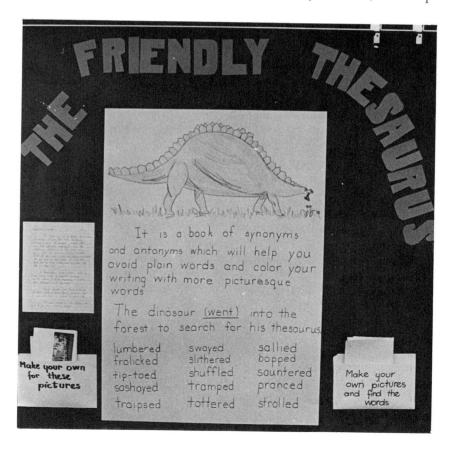

can be taken by teachers to alert children to new words or interesting language descriptions. Teachers must seek to reinforce the informal exposure and to consciously build language awareness.

Techniques for Promoting Vocabulary Development Through Literature

A chart of interesting words, descriptive phrases, and word pictures from literature can be kept. The teacher must initiate the discussion of language usage if awareness of language is to ensue. Books provide one of the best sources for stretching the imagination and expanding vocabulary. As children hear new stories and poems, they have an opportunity for assimilating new words into their listening and speaking vocabularies. The teacher's responsibility is to alert children before a story is read to listen for the interesting way an author describes a particular person or object, for all the words which describe a person's action, for all the words which describe sounds, and so forth.

A chart such as the following could be kept:

Interesting Language from Books

from *Listen, Rabbit**   "the rain was weeping down the eye of the window pane"

Word Pictures

from *Swimmy†*   "a lobster who moved about like a water moving machine"

After the reading of a story to children, a teacher may ask, "What did you notice about the word _____?" "What did it mean?" "How did the author use that word?" "Do you know any other words which he could have used which mean the same thing?" (It is better not to interrupt a story to explain a word or concept; explanations should occur either before or after the reading.)

The teacher may ask, "What was the most interesting or new word you heard in that story?" When one first grader was asked this question

---

* Aileen Fisher, *Listen, Rabbit* (New York: Crowell Collier & Macmillan, Inc., 1965).
† Lionni, *Swimmy*.

after listening to *The Camel Who Took a Walk* by Jack Tworkov,[19] he replied, "Flabbergasted." A notebook could be kept on the writing center table or in the reading center for additional examples from independent reading.

After reading a story, the teacher can ask, "What kind of person was _____?" or "How did _____ feel when _____?" Words such as *greedy, selfish, troublesome, frightened, unpleasant, understanding, sympathetic,* and *optimistic* might be discussed and added to the class word banks.

Children's literature materials which are directly related to vocabulary study are: *Sparkle and Spin* by Ann and Paul Rand,[20] *Words, Words, Words* by Mary O'Neill,[21] *A Hole Is to Dig* by Ruth Krauss,[22] and *Ounce, Dice, Trice* by Alistair Reid.[23]

Awareness of similes and metaphors can be begun even while children are in the pre-reading stage as they hear stories read aloud. The book, *Swimmy,* contains many examples of the interesting use of language through comparisons. Children can be asked to listen for how the lobster moved ("like a water-moving machine") or how the underwater flowers, the sea anemones, looked ("like pink palm trees swaying in the wind").[24] The book, *The Sun Is a Golden Earring,*[25] used in Chapter 4 contains excellent examples of similes and metaphors. This terminology is unimportant for children in the elementary level. However, the ability to use comparisons to communicate clearly, imaginatively, and expressively must be developed. The poem, "Cliche" in *It Doesn't Always Have to Rhyme* by Eve Merriam,[26] is excellent for having pupils identify comparisons. Children can extend the poem's idea to their own writing as they work with, "As warm as _____; as quiet as _____; as soft as _____; as quick as _____." Alvin Tresselt's *How Far Is Far?*[27] is another book which contains many imaginative descriptions which can be used to motivate children's writing.

---

[19] Jack Tworkov, *The Camel Who Took a Walk* (New York: E.P. Dutton & Co., Inc., 1951).

[20] Paul Rand and Ann Rand, *Sparkle and Spin* (New York: Harcourt, Brace & World, Inc., 1957).

[21] Mary O'Neill, *Words, Words, Words* (New York: Doubleday & Company, Inc., 1966).

[22] Ruth Krauss, *A Hole Is to Dig* (New York: Harper & Row, Publishers, 1952).

[23] Alistair Reid, *Ounce, Dice, Trice* (Boston: Little, Brown and Company, 1958).

[24] Lionni, *Swimmy.*

[25] Natalia Belting, *The Sun Is a Golden Earring* (New York: Holt, Rinehart & Winston, Inc., 1962).

[26] Eve Merriam, *It Doesn't Always Have to Rhyme* (New York: Atheneum Publishers, 1966).

[27] Alvin Tresselt, *How Far Is Far?* (New York: Parents' Magazine Press, 1964).

SUMMARY

Children's literature plays an important part throughout the language experience program in reading. Trade books of many types should be used to enrich the language and experience backgrounds of the pupils. Books can help to expand the reading and speaking vocabularies, to develop concepts, to provide training in purposeful listening as well as to develop the idea that reading is a pleasurable experience. Literature can add to a child's ability to use and understand language and to formulate in words what he sees, hears, feels, thinks, and imagines.

Literature is a language experience, but it is the teacher's responsibility to awaken the children's sensitivity to the language of literature. In so doing, the teacher must be aware of the examples of interesting language in children's books, must call the children's attention to these examples in a variety of ways, and must provide the stimulation and opportunities for children to develop their own creativity with language.

SUGGESTED READINGS

Arbuthnot, May Hill, *Children and Books*. Chicago: Scott, Foresman and Company, 1964. A basic reference source about children's literature, Arbuthnot's book contains much detailed information about types of literature, about authors, and about criteria for evaluating children's books.

Huck, Charlotte S. and Doris Y. Kuhn, *Children's Literature in the Elementary School*. New York: Holt, Rinehart, & Winston, Inc., 1968, Chapters 11, 12, 13. The chapters cited are concerned with the planned experiences with literature in the elementary classroom and with projects children can execute relating to their reading.

Whitehead, Robert, *Children's Literature: Strategies of Teaching*. Englewood Cliffs, N. J.: Prentice-Hall, Inc., 1968. Many activities with children's books are described in this publication. Many of the ideas can correlate with language experiences as children talk and write about their personal reading. Chapter 5 deals specifically with oral and written experiences with literature.

CHAPTER SEVEN

Pre-Reading Skills in the Language Experience Approach

Pre-reading, the stage of reading development which precedes the formal introduction to reading, is the base upon which future success and attitudes toward reading are built. Readiness for reading comes from a base of past experience, maturation, and training. A successful experience in reading from the initial stages of instruction should be the goal for every beginning reader. No sharp dividing line between pre-reading and beginning reading should exist, but instead there should be a gradual transition from one level of reading development to the next.

Language and experience are two important cornerstones on which readiness for reading is built. A language experience program can provide the foundation for a successful start in learning to read and can relate reading to the child's existing level of language development. Meaningful instruction in the skills of visual discrimination, auditory discrimination, letter names, and left-to-right progression across a line of print can be provided with pupil-composed materials in a language experience framework. Improving oral language facility in speaking and listening and developing an interest in reading are also concerns in the pre-reading period.

The language experience approach provides a natural transition from pre-reading to beginning reading as children are exposed to their oral language encoded in written form with personal and group experience stories. The language experience approach clearly demonstrates the relationship between spoken and written language and helps children recognize that printed words convey meaning. When experience stories are first used with children, they may be unable to recognize any words but gradually they learn to identify words, thus acquiring a sight vocabulary and moving into the beginning reading stage.

The language experience approach uses functional situations with oral and written language drawn from personal experiences to develop pre-reading skills. This approach to pre-reading is not dependent upon commercially prepared materials although a teacher may wish to combine language experience materials with selected commercial materials. This chapter is not intended to present a complete program of instruction in pre-reading. Rather, its intent is to describe how the language experience approach can be implemented to teach the important skills of the pre-reading period.

VISUAL DISCRIMINATION

Visual discrimination of likenesses and differences in letters and words is required in learning to read. Discrimination activities with letters and words have been found to be more valuable than activities with non-word forms.[1] Distinguishing similarities and differences between letters and between words is directly related to the perceptual tasks involved in reading whereas discriminating between pictures in a row or discriminating between geometric forms is not the same visual task as that required in reading.

The pupil-composed materials of the language experience approach offer many opportunities for teaching visual discrimination in a reading-type situation. For example, with the first experience charts in kindergarten and grade one, the teacher can have pupils match letter, word, phrase, and sentence cards to letters, words, phrases, and sentences on the charts. The teacher can direct the children to notice distinctive word features such as length and shape. This activity relates visual discrimination to a reading situation as children are working with meaningful content.

---

[1] Thomas A. Barrett, "The Relationship Between Measures of Pre-reading Visual Discrimination and First Grade Reading Achievement: A Review of the Literature," *Reading Research Quarterly*, I (Fall, 1965), 51.

In an activity such as writing daily plans with the class, the teacher can call the pupils' attention to the repetition of certain words. For example, plans such as the following could be written:

We will read.
We will write a story.
We will play outside.
We will have music.

The teacher can ask, "What do you notice about the first word in each line?" "What do you notice about the second word?" Word, phrase, and sentence cards can be used for matching.

In the above examples, the words have meaning for the students even though the children at the pre-reading level are not able to identify the words in other contexts. In the examples cited, the teacher said the word or phrase or sentence for the children to match. Pupils at the pre-reading level do not have to read words to respond to the task of matching visually. However, the teacher will use the word "read" in her explanations so that the children will realize that reading involves recognizing what the print represents.

Pupils' names provide another source for visual discrimination activities. A class roll chart with all the children's names can be used for matching activities. Each pupil will have an individual card with his name, and these cards can be matched to the names on the roll chart. Names with similar forms and letters can be grouped together to encourage fine discrimination. For example, names as similar as Larry and Harry, Tommy and Timmy, and Pat, Patricia, and Patrick should be grouped together.

Using pupils' names for other visual discrimination activities is also recommended. For example, a chart with horizontal rows of names can be made, and children can be directed to find all the names like the first one. The interest and motivation is usually high when pupil names are used. Names of objects in the room could also be used for teaching children to notice the first word in a line and then to identify all the other words in the line which are identical to the first one.

LEARNING LETTER NAMES

Knowledge of letter names correlates more highly with success in first grade reading than other measured factors.[2] Currently, readiness instruction is directing attention to teaching letter names before formal instruction in reading is begun. Knowing letter names is more than being able to recite the alphabet correctly. It is possible for a child to recite the alphabet and not be able to say the name of a letter when shown its printed form. Children should grasp the basic understanding that words are made up of letters and should be able to associate letter forms with letter names.

In the language experience approach, letter names can be taught in functional situations since children are constantly being exposed to letters in charts, in chalkboard writing, in their names, and in personal experience stories. The name chart and experience charts suggested for visual discrimination can also be used for letter matching activities. Each child should have an individual set of all upper and lower case letters to be used in the matching activities. The teacher can point to a name on the chart and ask the children to hold up the letter that they see at the beginning of that name. The name of the letter is stated by

---

[2] Guy L. Bond and Robert Dykstra, "The Cooperative Research Program in First-Grade Reading Programs," *Reading Research Quarterly*, II, No. 4 (1967), 116.

the teacher or children. In each case the name of the child should be read by the teacher so that the children realize the letter forms are used as parts of meaningful words.

The children can use their individual sets of upper and lower case letter cards for practice in learning letter names. Every child can respond if each has his own set of cards. For example, the teacher can say when pointing to a word on an experience chart or on the chalkboard, "This word begins with a capital M. Can all of you hold up your cards with capital M? Now can you find a little m?" The teacher praises the correct response and notes those children needing additional practice.

ABC books of children's literature can be read to children to promote interest in letters. A number of the attractively illustrated and imaginatively written ABC books, such as *Bruno Munari's ABC* by Bruno Munari,[3] *ABC of Cars and Trucks* by Anne Alexander,[4] and Wanda Gag's *The ABC Bunny*,[5] should be available in the classroom library corner for pupils to examine independently. Pupils can develop their own ABC books with illustrations for each of the letters. In developing the alphabet books, letter sounds will not be stressed since confusion can result at this stage if children are confronted with the numerous exceptions in the sound-letter relationships of the language. The emphasis in making class and individual ABC books is on the names and forms of letters.

Other activities can contribute to learning letter names. Learning to write can also direct children's attention to the names and forms of letters. As letters are used in visual discrimination training, the teacher may say, "Can you find all the l's in this line?" Boxes of letters may be available on the reading table, and children can be encouraged to build words to match the words in group and personal experience stories. Children can work in pairs in naming letters.

AUDITORY DISCRIMINATION

The ability to distinguish likenesses and differences in the sounds of spoken words is a skill important for success in initial reading. Phonics instruction begins with gross auditory discrimination in the pre-reading stage. Durrell states that attention to the auditory factor of distinguish-

---

[3] Bruno Munari, *Bruno Munari's ABC* (New York: The World Publishing Company, 1960).

[4] Anne Alexander, *ABC of Cars and Trucks* (New York: Doubleday & Company, Inc., 1956).

[5] Wanda Gag, *The ABC Bunny* (New York: Coward-McCann, Inc., 1933).

ing the separate sounds of spoken words is the most neglected subskill in readiness training.[6]

In initial reading instruction attention is given to the *association* of a sound with the printed letter symbol. Prior to that type of instruction, the ability to discriminate similarities and differences in sounds is particularly important in both beginning and rhyming sounds. Numerous opportunities for auditory discrimination grow out of language experience activities.

As group experience charts are written with pupils, attention can be directed to words on a chart which begin with the same sound. For example, with the chart on page 29, the teacher might say, "Listen as I say these words: carrots, cabbage; go get. Listen for the first sound in them."

The name chart described on page 83 can also be used for auditory discrimination as the teacher can ask pupils to listen for similarities in the beginning sounds of several names such as Jack, Johnny, Joyce. Groups of three names, two of which have the same beginning sound and one with a different beginning sound can be used as children are asked to indicate which two names begin alike.

In personal experience stories, teachers can point out to a child that two or more words begin with the same sound and have him say the words to hear the sound. Work on rhyming words is also included when they appear in the group and individual experience stories.

Research has established that culturally disadvantaged children are deficient in auditory discrimination upon entering school.[7] These disadvantaged children who come from a very noisy environment have learned to shut out all sounds and have not learned to distinguish the characteristics of any sounds. Intensive, specific training is recommended. For children who are unable to distinguish between letter sounds in spoken words, more gross auditory discrimination may be advisable.

To develop an awareness of sound in the environment before progressing to letter sounds, children's literature books such as *The Listening Walk* by Paul Showers[8] and the series of "Noisy Books" by Margaret

---

[6] Donald D. Durrell, "Learning Factors in Beginning Reading," in *Teaching Young Children to Read*, ed. Warren G. Cutts (Washington, D.C.: U.S. Office of Education, 1964), p. 72.

[7] Martin Deutsch, "The Disadvantaged Child and the Learning Process," in *Education in Depressed Areas*, ed. A. Harry Passow (New York: Bureau of Publications, Teachers College, Columbia University, 1963), p. 171.

[8] Paul Showers, *The Listening Walk* (New York: Crowell Collier & Macmillan, Inc., 1961).

Wise Brown[9] are very helpful. Listening activities in the classroom or taking a listening walk can be used. Additional suggestions for improving awareness of sounds can be found in *Listening Aids Through the Grades* by David and Elizabeth Russell.[10]

LEFT-TO-RIGHT DIRECTION

Following a line of print from left-to-right is a requirement of the reading act. This skill must be carefully taught, and the correct orientation to the printed page must be established in the pre-reading period. Developing the habit of observing printed words and sentences from left-to-right should be a major focus of the skill training of the pre-reading period.

Language experience materials can be used to demonstrate left-to-right sequence in reading situations. In other words, left-to-right is taught not by observing rows of pictures but with printed letters and words, thereby relating the training to the task needed in reading. The major advantage of the language experience approach activities for teaching left-to-right progression is the natural relationship of this skill to the actual reading situations.

As the teacher writes and reads plans, she will show left-to-right direction by telling pupils that in writing she always starts at the left side and goes to the right. As she reads she will move her hand from left-to-right under the words. In the reading of all group experience stories, the left-to-right direction is demonstrated by the teacher with her hand or a pointer. As pupils match cards to a chart, the teacher shows left-to-right direction. In working with personal experience stories, the teacher can show individual pupils how to read print from left-to-right. As pupils underline words on the board, on a chart, or in a personal experience story, the teacher again encourages left-to-right progression. As pupils learn to do manuscript writing, left-to-right direction is also taught. Of course, game-type activities with left and right directions such as "Simon Says" and "Looby Loo" can also be used.

ORAL LANGUAGE

Increasing oral language facility is another concern in the pre-reading program since the ability to comprehend and express ideas through oral

---

[9] Margaret Wise Brown, *The City Noisy Book* (New York: Harper & Row, Publishers, 1939).

[10] David Russell and Elizabeth Russell, *Listening Aids Through the Grades* (New York: Bureau of Publications, Teachers College, Columbia University, 1959).

language contributes to meaningful reading. There must be something to talk about, but, while starting with pupil backgrounds, the teacher must not limit the exposure of pupils to only that language and those experiences which they now possess. It is the teacher's obligation to extend the experience background and to develop language competency. In the language experience approach with the integration of speaking, listening, reading, and writing, oral language experiences receive considerable attention.

Children must be *encouraged* to talk in situations where they feel free to express themselves regardless of their level of language development and regardless of their language patterns. Children must be *encouraged* to talk when stimuli for conversation and discussion are ample and ever-changing. Children must be *encouraged* to talk where pupil talk is regarded as more important than teacher talk. Children must be *encouraged* to talk in situations where they are exposed to new experiences, new vocabulary, and new thoughts through tapes, stories, trips, films, and pictures. Children must be *encouraged* to talk in an environment where their talk is the basis for other language experiences as they compose group and personal experience stories and class and individual books, as they listen to the ideas of others and state their own, and as they read their ideas.

PROMOTING INTEREST IN READING

Before formal instruction in reading is begun, it is important that children develop a desire to read. Children who have been read to at home or in nursery school and kindergarten have experienced pleasurable contacts with books. For those children who have not had such contacts, providing opportunities to hear stories and to examine the attractive picture-story books is even more important. The most effective means for developing an interest in reading is through exposure to interesting children's literature materials. Realizing that meaning comes from the printed page and that reading is an enjoyable experience are understandings conveyed through hearing stories read aloud. Every classroom should contain an attractive library corner, and every classroom should feature a daily period of story reading by the teacher.

The personal pride that results from pupil authorship also has a favorable effect on pupil interest. The group and individual experience stories written with children in the pre-reading and beginning reading stages should foster enthusiasm for reading since the content is of high interest to pupils. If the introduction to reading occurs in a functional situation, interest should be inherent in the situation. Success with the pupil-composed materials should also have a favorable effect on attitude and interest.

SUMMARY

Pre-reading instruction in visual discrimination, letter names, auditory discrimination, left-to-right progression, language development, and interest in reading can be approached from a language experience framework. Particular emphasis is placed on encouraging oral language development since this is the base from which other language experiences grow. Children's oral language forms the basis of pupil-produced materials which can be used for skill instruction in pre-reading.

In the language experience approach, the pre-reading stage blends gradually into the beginning reading stage through the use of group experience charts and personal experience stories. The language experience approach to pre-reading illustrates the relationship between spoken and written language. Pre-reading training in the language experience approach develops skills needed for beginning reading in a reading-like situation with functional, pupil-developed materials rather than with artificial materials remote from children's experiences. Pre-reading and beginning reading are introduced in a situation which fosters success and healthy attitudes toward self and toward learning.

SUGGESTED READINGS

Monroe, Marion and Bernice Rogers, *Foundations for Reading*. Chicago: Scott, Foresman and Company, 1964. Detailed discussions of pre-reading skills and of instructional techniques are included in this source.

Howes, Virgil and Helen Darrow, *Reading and the Elementary School Child*. New York: The Macmillan Company, 1968. In Chapter 4 of this collection of articles about reading, issues in pre-reading are discussed.

Lee, Dorris M. and R. Van Allen, *Learning to Read Through Experience*. New York: Appleton-Century-Crofts, 1963. This basic source on the language experience approach gives many examples of the transition from pre-reading to initial reading instruction. The philosophy of the language experience approach as a natural introduction to reading is a basic theme of this book.

CHAPTER EIGHT

Teaching Reading Skills in the Language Experience Approach

All of the theory and techniques of the preceding chapters were concerned with teaching children to read effectively. Because the language experience approach is so concerned with reading as communication through language symbols, the direct teaching of specific reading skills may not receive sufficient attention for several reasons. First, since the language experience approach is built from pupils' oral language, the dimension of skill instruction may not be clearly recognized. Second, since the language experience approach is an integrated one with the language skills taught *through* pupil composition and experiences with spoken and written language, a teacher may not be clear about the types and amounts of direct skill instruction which should be offered. Third, the language experience approach is not one with a clear, systematic sequence of learning according to a predetermined guide. The purpose of this chapter is to identify needed reading skills and to suggest means of incorporating skill instruction in the language experience framework by discussing word attack, comprehension, and oral reading skills.

WORD ATTACK SKILLS IN THE LANGUAGE EXPERIENCE APPROACH

Any reading program must teach children methods of attacking unfamiliar words quickly and independently. Each teacher must identify the content of word attack,

89

provide both direct and incidental instruction, and evaluate children's learning in this area. In order to have a strong and well-rounded reading program while following a language experience plan of reading instruction, it is recommended that the teacher follow a systematic, definite program in word attack skills in addition to the other language experience activities. Flexible grouping for skill instruction in the language experience approach is recommended since groups will be formed on the basis of need for a common skill and will either be disbanded or modified in composition as needs change. Teachers can follow checklists of skills in phonics and structural analysis and keep a record for each child, to note when a skill has been mastered and to indicate those skills which need to be learned. Many teachers keep a notebook or file box of informal observations about each child's reading performance.

The language experience approach does offer an excellent means for reinforcing skill training in functional situations. The language experience approach can teach skills as needed by pupils in their independent reading and writing. Pupils' language in the group and individual stories and in their word banks will provide examples to be used in the skill instruction. The skills needed for independence in word attack are configuration, phonics, structural analysis, context clues, and use of the dictionary.

In Chart I, the reader will find an overview of the content of phonics and structural analysis which can be used for recording a child's progress. Pre-reading skills in letter name knowledge, visual discrimination, and auditory discrimination are included. Space is provided for recording when a skill is taught and when it is mastered. The checklist is written with descriptions of the child's behavior which would demonstrate skill competency. For more complete discussions of word attack content, see the suggested readings at the end of the chapter.

CHART I   WORD ATTACK CHECKLIST

CHILD _____

PRE-READING

Can auditorily discriminate between likeness and difference in beginning sounds

          Taught   Mastered
        _____   _____

Can auditorily discriminate by recognizing rhyming words

       Taught   Mastered

_____   _____

Can identify letter forms by name

       Taught   Mastered

_____   _____

Can visually discriminate by matching capital letter forms

       Taught   Mastered

_____   _____

Can visually discriminate by matching lower-case letter forms

       Taught   Mastered

_____   _____

Can visually discriminate by matching word forms

       Taught   Mastered

_____   _____

CONSONANTS

Single Consonants: b, hard c, soft c, d, f, hard g, soft g, h, j, k, l, m, n, p, qu, r, s, t, v, w, x, y, z

Can identify in initial position in words

       Taught   Mastered

_____   _____

Can identify in medial position in words

       Taught   Mastered

_____   _____

Can identify in final position in words

       Taught   Mastered

_____   _____

Can substitute consonants to attack new words

    in initial position (Jack to back)

       Taught   Mastered

_____   _____

in final position (bed to beg)
Taught   Mastered

_____   _____

Consonant blends: l blends: bl, cl, fl, gl, pl, sl, spl
r blends: br, cr, dr, fr, gr, pr, tr, scr, spr, str, thr
s blends: sc, sk, sm, sn, sp, st, sw, str

Can identify *l* blends in spoken and written words
Taught   Mastered

_____   _____

Can identify *r* blends in spoken and written words
Taught   Mastered

_____   _____

Can identify *s* blends in spoken and written words
Taught   Mastered

_____   _____

Can substitute blends to attack new words
Taught   Mastered

_____   _____

Consonant Digraphs: sh, ch, wh, th (both voiced and unvoiced)

Can identify in spoken and written words
Taught   Mastered

_____   _____

Can substitute digraphs to attack new words
Taught   Mastered

_____   _____

VOWELS

Long, short, r-controlled sounds

Can recognize long vowel sounds in spoken and written words
Taught   Mastered

_____   _____

Can recognize short vowel sounds in spoken and written words
Taught   Mastered

_____   _____

Can recognize r-controlled vowel sounds in spoken and written words
Taught   Mastered

Other vowel sounds: long oo, short oo, oi and oy diphthong, ou and ow
diphthong, y as long i and long e.

Can recognize long and short oo in spoken and written words
    Taught   Mastered

———————   ———————

Can recognize oi and oy diphthong in spoken and written words
    Taught   Mastered

———————   ———————

Can recognize y as long i and long e in spoken and written words
    Taught   Mastered

———————   ———————

Vowel generalizations: The generalizations which apply to these key
    words 1. gō, 2. gĕt, 3. rāin, 4. rīde

Can state and apply generalization No. 1.
    Taught   Mastered

———————   ———————

Can state and apply generalization No. 2.
    Taught   Mastered

———————   ———————

Can state and apply generalization No. 3.
    Taught   Mastered

———————   ———————

Can state and apply generalization No. 4.
    Taught   Mastered

———————   ———————

SYLLABICATION

Generalizations: 1. vccv 2. vcv 3. c + le = last syllable
      lad/der lā/dy   lā/dle

Can state and apply generalization No. 1.
    Taught   Mastered

———————   ———————

Can state and apply generalization No. 2.
    Taught   Mastered

———————   ———————

Can state and apply generalization No. 3.
Taught   Mastered

———————   ———————

Can apply vowel generalizations to determine vowel sounds in syllables.
Taught   Mastered

———————   ———————

STRUCTURAL ANALYSIS

Compound words, contractions, roots, prefixes, and suffixes.
Can recognize and attack compound words
Taught   Mastered

———————   ———————

Can recognize and attack contractions
Taught   Mastered

———————   ———————

Can recognize and attack words with roots, prefixes, and suffixes
(Teachers can list specific prefixes and suffixes)
Taught   Mastered

———————   ———————

Structural Changes: 1. Drop silent e (ride to riding) 2. double consonant
(hop to hopping) 3. y to i (candy to candies)
Can read and spell words following generalization No. 1.
Taught   Mastered

———————   ———————

Can read and spell words following generalization No. 2.
Taught   Mastered

———————   ———————

Can read and spell words following generalization No. 3.
Taught   Mastered

———————   ———————

Configuration   Configuration clues about the general shape or form of
a word are some of the first techniques used in reading as children learn
to recognize words. When children begin to read experience stories and
add words to the word banks, they are using configuration clues as they
acquire a sight vocabulary. For specific instruction in configuration, the
teacher may provide practice during group experience story activities.
Pupils match word cards to cards on the chart, find words that begin a
particular way, and circle or frame certain words. These procedures are

really an extension of visual discrimination begun in the pre-reading period.

For individual work with configuration, the personal experience stories and word banks offer excellent materials for practice. A child can match words in the word bank to the words in his stories, he can underline known words, he can find words with similar configuration such as *can* and *car*, and *look* and *book*, and he can compare likenesses and differences in words. The goal of such configuration practice and exposure to word forms is to add to the sight vocabulary, the stock of words recognized instantly when seen in print. Any good reader must have a large sight vocabulary, and the teacher must seek to constantly enlarge children's reading vocabularies through many language experience activities.

Phonics   In working with phonics in the language experience approach, an analytic approach which refers to studying speech sounds in whole words rather than studying single sounds in isolation is preferred. In an analytic approach, known sight words are used in developing an understanding of the phoneme-grapheme (sound-symbol) relationships of the language.

In the teaching of the association of a sound with its printed counterpart, the teacher must provide auditory and visual experience with the sound and letter form and must demonstrate the application of the phoneme-grapheme relationship to attack an unfamiliar word in context. Since phonics instruction aims to equip children with a tool for attacking unfamiliar words, the application step must be stressed. For example, in working with the inital sound of "m," the teacher may group several children together and ask them to find all of the words in their word banks which begin with "m." The instruction will include hearing the sound of "m" as the words are said aloud. Then, several words familiar to all the pupils will be listed so that children can see the visual form of "m" in whole word forms. Then some sentences can be written with a new word beginning with "m" in each sentence. The children can attack these words by using the phonic and context clues. Examples might be, "When it is cold, you wear *mittens*," or "The *milk* is white." The children are told that they know all the words except the one beginning with "m" and are told to think of a word which would make sense in each sentence.

Words which are already know by children can be used to illustrate the consonant substitution technique for attacking new words. The teacher might say, "You know the word ten. What word do you have if the t is changed to an m?" Additional examples such as *bat* to *mat*, *six* to *mix* could be used.

A similar procedure can be followed in teaching the sound-symbol relationships of the other consonants, the consonant blends, the consonant digraphs, and the vowel sounds.

Structural Analysis Structural analysis involves attacking unfamiliar words by analyzing word parts. Children must be taught to look for compound words, roots, prefixes, suffixes, contractions, and known syllables. The last part of the word-attack checklist (Chart I) lists the major skills of structural analysis. Flexible grouping of pupils for direct instruction is recommended while working with the checklist content.

These skills can be taught through examples from the personal and group experience stories and the word banks. Structural analysis of prefixes and suffixes should be illustrated in sentence context. In working with prefixes and suffixes, emphasis must be on meaning not just on form or pronunciation. It is more valuable for a child to use meaningful sentences to decide whether *wish, wishes, wished,* or *wishing* is appropriate instead of merely writing the word *wish* with endings since it is only in a sentence context that a child will know which form is appropriate.

Botel describes a discovery procedure for developing the understanding of generalizations. Children are given auditory and visual examples with a particular pattern. They are then directed to observe the pattern through careful teacher questioning, to collect words which follow the pattern, and to formulate the appropriate generalization for the pattern.[1]

For example, if children were working with the structural change generalization in which the final consonant is doubled in a word having a consonant-vowel-consonant (*hop*) pattern before adding an ending, the discovery procedure would work as follows: The teacher could write several pairs of sentences such as, "Jack will bat next," "He has a good batting average," or "The car will stop at the light," "The car has stopped." She could then ask, "Can you find the root word in *batting?*" "Does the ending begin with a vowel or a consonant?" "What is added to the root word before adding the ending?" "Look at the last three letters of the root words." Children should note the consonant-vowel-consonant pattern of the root words. They can be asked to find words in their reading which fit this pattern. In the inductive learning of the discovery procedure, the generalization is stated by the children after specific examples are studied.

The preceding procedure is helpful regardless of the instructional approach in reading. However, in the language experience approach, the distinctive characteristic is the selection of words from the children's writing. The above procedure can be applied to the examples listed in Chart I for vowel generalizations, syllabication generalizations, and structural analysis.

Context Context clues in word attack refer to the use of surrounding reading material to determine the meaning and pronunciation of an unfamiliar word. Because the language experience approach works with meaningful materials in sentence and story contexts, the use of context clues can be easily taught and applied. As children first learn to read their spoken language, the use of context reading is evident. When a child does not know a word while reading a sentence the teacher may say, "If you remember the rest of what you said, you may be able to figure out the word."

Contextual closure exercises which omit one word from a sentence can be developed with sentences from language experience stories. For example, a teacher may take sentences from a group experience story, write them on the board, on a transparancy for the overhead projector,

---

[1] Morton Botel, *How to Teach Reading* (Chicago: Follett Publishing Company, 1963), pp. 43-45.

or on another chart. She can then ask the children if they can select from the words written on word cards or on the board which word belongs in a particular sentence. Closure activities can be done in the same manner with individual stories and with words from word banks. Small groups can be formed with children reading sentences from their individual stories, leaving out a word, and asking the group members to suggest the appropriate word. Such activity helps the concept of synonyms and can extend both the speaking and reading vocabularies. The use of context clues is also combined with phonic and structural clues in attacking unfamiliar words.

Dictionary Functional and informal dictionary activities can be included in the language experience framework. The interest in word study which was a theme of Chapter 5 should encourage children to be enthusiastic about using dictionaries. As children read and write independently, they should be encouraged to use the dictionary as an aid to meaning, spelling, and pronunciation. At every grade level in the elementary school, dictionaries should always be available for reference in the classroom writing center and reading corner. A number of easy, attractively-illustrated picture dictionaries are now available for beginning readers. Beyond the primary levels, other commercial dictionaries can be provided.

All of the word bank experiences with alphabetizing and word meaning should facilitate dictionary study. Word banks can lead to the development of class and individual dictionaries as children write definitions and alphabetize and list words in a notebook in dictionary form. The concept of multiple meanings can be developed through discussion of the words in word banks, and children can compose a group bank of "Words with More than One Meaning."

Using alphabetizing in functional situations with language experience activities can be included in the total program. For example, in one primary class, the children made a class dictionary of names, addresses, and telephone numbers. The original purpose was to have a list for sending Christmas and Valentine cards. The teacher explained that directories are alphabetized according to the last name. The games and activities listed in the pamphlet, *Fun With Words* by Scott, Foresman and Company[2] and the activities suggested at the beginning of the Scott, Foresman *Junior* and *Beginning Thorndike-Barnhart Dictionaries* can make the teaching of dictionary skills lively and interesting.

---

[2] *Fun With Words* (Glenview, Ill.: Scott, Foresman and Company, 1962).

COMPREHENSION SKILLS IN THE LANGUAGE EXPERIENCE APPROACH

Instruction in reading must promote thinking as children react to content. Without comprehension, reading is of little value. In the language experience approach, the communication of meaning is present in the three steps of producing reading materials, and one of the major advantages of this approach in the beginning reading stage is the use of material with high meaning. However, not all comprehension skills can be taught through pupil-composed materials. While children understand the meaning of their own stories, care must be exercised to ensure that children are equipped to derive meaning from materials written by others. Exposure to many types of materials is essential, especially beyond the initial stages of reading. Children should be given numerous opportunities to read the stories of other children and to react through discussion in group situations to the meaning of various materials.

In teaching reading as a thinking process, teachers need to require children to read beyond the literal level. Children should search for deeper meanings as they interpret an author's words in light of personal experiences and as they seek answers to questions which involve more than recalling facts. Careful questioning by the teacher on various levels of comprehension is essential. The detailed descriptions of questions by Sanders in *Classroom Questions* is particularly helpful. Teachers will find extensive discussions of teaching comprehension included in a number of textbooks on reading methodology. (See Suggested Readings.)

All of the comments stated throughout this book on the importance of communication in the reading process and in the language experience framework of learning and teaching are relevant to teaching comprehension in reading. Attention to increasing vocabulary and to facilitating expression in spoken and written language contribute to the interpretation of reading material. Exposure to literature read orally also requires interpretation of language symbols and enriches the knowledge background. As children react to each others' writing positively and constructively, they are actively involved in obtaining meaning from print.

ORAL READING IN THE LANGUAGE EXPERIENCE APPROACH

Helping children communicate through expressive oral reading is another concern of the teacher of elementary reading skills. Oral reading in the elementary school should occur in functional situations and should not be done in a mechanical or routine manner.

The language experience approach which uses children's spoken language presents an excellent means for helping children realize that print represents their speech. Children can realize that in reading they must supply the intonation of spoken language. From the time of the recording of the first group and individual experience stories, the teacher demonstrates fluent oral reading when he reads the stories to the children. Although some teachers tend to read in such a way as to distort the speech patterns with their desire to have children observe individual words carefully, word-by-word emphasis is to be avoided. Children should employ expressive reading naturally as they read print which was originally an oral story. Gradually discussion of punctuation clues for intonation will occur through the individual and group pupil-composed materials. As the teacher points out, "This is the end of your thought, so we'll put a period or a dot. The next line is a new sentence, so it will begin with a capital letter." Instruction of this nature should not overshadow the writing and reading experience but can be included occasionally.

The language experience approach has distinct advantages for teaching oral reading. Oral reading is taught from the beginning stages as a way of making print sound like the spoken language instead of working with unnatural word-by-word recitation of controlled vocabulary materials. Sentence patterns which are already in the child's speech form the basis for reading words in meaningful sentence patterns with the characteristic juncture, pitch, and stress normally employed in speech. For disadvantaged children, the use of their own experience stories is particularly important since reading textbooks do not use their sentence patterns making the task of reading especially difficult.

Meaningful oral reading related to language experience activities can occur as small, flexible groups are formed for sharing stories. As pupils read their own and their classmates' stories, they can practice effective oral reading. Children can record their stories, and the tapes can be replayed for personal evaluation of the oral reading.

Silent reading should receive greater emphasis than oral reading since too much emphasis on the latter can be detrimental to the development of a satisfactory rate of silent reading. Since oral reading without meaning is a barrier to comprehension, and since the majority of reading tasks require silent reading, such emphasis is essential. However, oral reading should be taught since it can require all the skills of silent reading in addition to those of oral communication. In the language experience activities as well as in experiences with other reading materials, children should first read silently that which they are asked to read aloud. Oral reading serves as a diagnostic tool for the teacher as she notes indications of difficulty and analyzes patterns of errors or particular weaknesses.

SUMMARY

Effective teaching of reading must include the teaching of word attack, comprehension, and oral reading. Since the creative, communicative, personal, and functional attributes of the language experience approach are so important, direct teaching of skills may be neglected. Many functional situations in the language experience approach may be utilized to illustrate or to reinforce particular skills. However, direct instruction in skills is essential in a strong reading program. It is recommended that the teacher offer both direct and indirect skill instruction in the areas discussed in this chapter.

SUGGESTED READINGS

Barbe, Walter, *An Educator's Guide to Personalized Reading Instruction*. Englewood Cliffs, N.J.: Prentice-Hall, Inc., 1961. Barbe has compiled checklists of reading skills which are extremely helpful to the teacher in keeping records of children's mastery of specific skills.

Bond, Guy L. and Eva B. Wagner, *Teaching the Child to Read*. New York: The Macmillan Company, 1966. In Chapters 9 and 10, basic comprehension skills are identified and discussed.

Botel, Morton, *How to Teach Reading*. Chicago: Follett Publishing Company, 1963. Step-by-step teaching procedures are outlined with specific examples. A brief overview of the content of word attack is given and the use of questions for developing comprehension is clearly explained.

Heilman, Arthur, *Phonics in Proper Perspective*. Columbus: Charles E. Merrill Publishing Company, 1968. This paperback book contains an overview of phonics content in reading as well as clear procedures for teaching word attack skills.

Sanders, Norris M., *Classroom Questions*. New York: Harper & Row, Publishers, 1966. A classification of types of questions is clearly elaborated. Using questions of the types discussed in this source can promote depth in reading comprehension.

Wilson, Robert M. and MaryAnne Hall, *Programmed Word Attack for Teachers*. Columbus: Charles E. Merrill Publishing Company, 1968. For the teacher unfamiliar with the content of word attack, this programmed text provides a comprehensive overview.

CHAPTER NINE

The Language Experience Classroom

Reading as a language experience has been described, and the instructional dimensions have been explored in the preceding chapters. Now, in summary, certain overall concerns of the teacher who wishes to employ this approach are examined in this chapter. What is the classroom environment like? How is the language experience classroom organized? How is learning evaluated in the language experience approach?

THE CLASSROOM ENVIRONMENT
FOR THE
LANGUAGE EXPERIENCE APPROACH

The most important single influence on learning in any given classroom is the teacher. The attitudes of the teacher, his rapport with children, his arrangement of stimuli for learning, and his knowledge and skill are hard to measure objectively but are extremely influential in his effectiveness.

The author feels that the attributes of the language experience approach discussed in Chapter 1 and the attitudes identified in Chapter 2 must be internalized by the teacher. To demonstrate these attributes and attitudes, a teacher must create a classroom climate of acceptance with stimuli for creativity. Teachers must

103

believe that children can learn through personal involvement in situations requiring communication and that children's ability to use language effectively can be developed through the use of *their* language as the base of teaching and learning.

Teachers' expectations of children's performance affect learning. The experiment reported in *Pygmallion in the Classroom* demonstrated conclusively that children will perform according to teachers' expectations.[1] The authors of that book randomly selected 20 per cent of an elementary school population and told the teachers of these children that they would show unusual intellectual growth. The children thus identified did show significant gains as measured by I.Q. tests given at the end of the experiment.

The language experience classroom should provide ideas and materials for worthwhile independent activities in the language arts. Learning centers offering planned reinforcement of specific learning where children can pursue individual interests are featured in increasing numbers in today's classrooms. Teachers are concerned about the time needed for language experience instruction. Classroom organization which uses language experience activities for independent learning adds considerably to the effectiveness of the approach since much learning can occur in the self-directed activities. Additional experiences with a particular skill or topic can be done independently in the learning centers. Learning centers offer activities which are not required or standardized for all children but which serve as an opportunity for encouraging and extending pupil interests. Three learning centers of particular importance in the implementation of the language experience approach are a reading center, a listening center, and a writing center.

Reading Center.   The reading center should foster wide independent reading as materials of a variety of types and levels are available to students. The center should be an inviting place with attractive displays and comfortable chairs or rugs. The children's literature materials in the center will lead to creative writing and other language experience activities. Pupil displays of art work and writing correlated with literature should be evident here. The reading center, too, is a place for displaying children's independent writing in the form of individual and class books. Children should participate in the arrangement of the center and can assume partial responsibility for the displays of their work. Many of the ideas suggested in Chapters 3 and 4 can be used in the reading center.

---

[1] Robert Rosenthal and Lenore Jacobson, *Pygmallion in the Classroom* (New York: Holt, Rinehart & Winston, Inc., 1968).

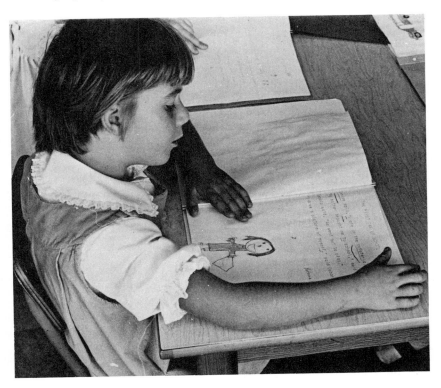

Listening Center. A listening center will include a tape recorder, record player, and sets of head phones and plug-in jacks. Teachers find that tapes and records which can be used by children with little or no teacher direction are extremely useful both for direct instruction and for independent learning. Children's literature selections can be taped and replayed by individuals or small groups. Children can record their creative stories. Motivation for meaningful oral reading is provided as pupils tape materials for their classmates and for other classes and grades. As children find enjoyable passages in their independent reading, they can tape these. Teachers can play the tapes to evaluate pupils' oral reading skills.

For directed lessons with listening center materials, teachers can tape directions to correlate with a particular lesson and can have children follow directions from the tape without requiring the presence of the teacher. Certain phonics lessons are quite appropriate for taped presentation. Publishers now have a quantity of tapes and records to correlate with all content areas. Also popular for listening centers are "read-along" materials which include books so children can watch the print while hearing the story on the tape. Many teachers are making their own "read-along" materials using favorite literature selections and pupil-composed language experience stories.

Writing Center. Another important center is the writing center which should serve as a stimulus for personal writing and for additional independent activities directly correlated with the language experience instruction. The writing center should include such essentials as commercial and class picture dictionaries, class word banks, pencils, crayons, paper, and the like. Pictures and objects can be placed in this center to stimulate creative writing. As in all centers, ideas will need to be changed frequently to maintain interest. The materials in the writing center can provide an excellent means for following-up previous language lessons or activities. For example, if a class is studying descriptive words, the teacher can reinforce this content by asking the children to write descriptive words for objects or pictures in the writing center or to write a story using descriptive words. The writing center should serve as an invitation to write, not as a required assignment for pupils.

   Of course at the very early stages of reading development, the activities in the writing center will need considerable structure; but as children grow in reading power, less help will be necessary. Beginning readers may wish to practice handwriting by copying a group experience story, but children should not be required to do this. In the very early stage of learning to read, model sentences can be used in the writing center with some element of word choice. For example, to provide practice in reading and writing color words, objects and pictures along with word cards for each object and picture can be placed in the writing center. The model sentence could be, "A _____ is yellow," with pictures of pencils, paper, bananas, pears, the sun, and butter. Children could write a sentence, illustrate it, and use it for a group book. Other model sentence ideas might be "Round things" or "I like to _____," with pictures and phrases such as "ride my bike," "play football," "play with dolls," or "run in the leaves."

   In Chapter 4, the teaching of creative writing was discussed. A teacher can follow-up the direct instruction in types and techniques of writing with examples in the writing center. For example, if a class were working on tall tales, the writing center could feature examples from both children's writings and literature. Pictures or topics for additional tall tales could be suggested as an independent activity. This use of the writing center could be adapted for each type and technique of writing.

A popular idea for a writing center is the use of pictures with questions and captions to stimulate writing. Some suggestions are:

Can you write an animal story?
Can you write an imaginary story?
Can you write a story about snow?
Can you make up a surprise ending for these pictures?
What descriptive words can you use to describe how the child in this picture felt?

The ideas for the writing center are inexhaustible since the illustrations, captions, and questions can be extremely varied.

CLASSROOM ORGANIZATION IN THE LANGUAGE EXPERIENCE APPROACH

In facilitating instruction in the language experience approach, whole group, small group, and individual learning situations are utilized. While individualization of instruction is a prime consideration, group instruction is desirable for certain experiences and, in many cases, is more efficient than individual instruction. However, the individual nature of the language experience approach is one of its major attributes and individual response of a personal and unique nature is to be encouraged constantly. Large group experiences can often lead to different individual activities for each child as he creates his personal reading materials.

Literature experiences, group experience stories, planning sessions, and creative writing can occur with a total class group. Certain language activities involving word banks can also be used with large groups. Group interaction through discussion is valuable since in this way children learn to be careful listeners, and they learn to compromise.

Small group instruction is desirable for the sharing of personal writing, for instruction in skills, and for directed instruction in reading for those pupils with the same reading level. Small groups can be temporary and disbanded when no longer needed. Pupils can work together in small groups without teacher direction as they share writing, talk about words, and discuss their independent reading.

Children can work in pairs or in teams. These pairs or teams can read orally to each other, can work together in building sentences with the word banks, and can share their individual stories. Small groups can be formed on an interest basis as children who have written or have read materials on a particular topic share their information. Projects on which several children work together provide another situation for small group instruction.

Individual instruction is offered when a teacher records a child's personal story and when selected re-reading activities are conducted with the story. (See page 33.) Using the individualized reading approach in conjunction with the language experience approach is favored by many teachers. The individual pupil-teacher conference is utilized in both the individualized and language experience approaches to instruction. In the conference situation the teacher observes a child's reading needs, suggests material for future reading, and provides needed skill instruction.

When·organizing a language experience instructional program, the teacher should look at the total language program, not just at the reading program. The language experience activities described in this book rest upon a philosophy of integration of all the language arts.

EVALUATION IN THE LANGUAGE EXPERIENCE APPROACH

Evaluation is a continuous process and is a part of all curriculum experiences. Informal evaluation will occur in everyday situations with spoken and written language. More formal evaluation will come in the form of record keeping and standardized testing. In the language experience approach, the teacher must evaluate children's learning in reading and the other language arts in terms of the instructional goals discussed in Chapter 2. Those goals can be stated in question form as guides for teacher evaluation of reading and language programs. Are children growing in their ability to use reading as a medium of communication? Are reading vocabularies increasing? Are they developing favorable attitudes and genuine interest in reading? In their total language development are children able to demonstrate progress in the goals stated in Applegate (to use words responsibly, to think clearly, to listen imaginatively, to speak effectively, to read thoughtfully, to write creatively, to use mechanics powerfully, to regard good English respectively, to be aware of the best [literature])[2]? The teacher should ask, too, whether children are responding creatively in the language experience activities.

---

[2] Mauree Applegate, *Easy in English* (Evanston, Illinois: Row, Peterson and Company, 1960), p. 8.

FINAL SUMMARY

Teaching reading as a language experience rests on a philosophy of personal, communicative, creative, and functional learning and teaching. Instruction is built on children's existing level of language expression as speech is encoded with written symbols and as they read the written record of their spoken thoughts.

Language study in speaking, listening, reading, and writing occurs in situations which contain and stimulate a high degree of pupil involvement. Pupil-developed materials are central to instruction in the language experience framework. The language experience approach is used as a bridge from pre-reading to beginning reading, as a component of a balanced reading program in combination with other approaches, as a means of reaching the discouraged remedial reader, and as a means of providing materials relevant to disadvantaged children.

The instructional program stresses creative writing, vocabulary development, and literary experiences in a classroom based on flexibility, receptiveness, and stimulation. The classroom setting includes learning centers where children can pursue independent language activities. Individual, small group, and total group instruction are included in the language experiences. As teachers evaluate the children's ability to communicate through spoken and written language, they base their evaluation on the goals described in Chapter 2.

Index

Index